LIFE IN JENERAL

LIFE IN JENERAL

A JOYFUL GUIDE TO ORGANIZING YOUR HOME AND CREATING THE SPACE FOR WHAT MATTERS MOST

HarperOne

An Imprint of HarperCollinsPublishers

This one's for you, Dad.

For all the ways you continually

chose to make space for me.

For showing me that life is meant

for loving people.

And for proving that a glass of wine

and a good laugh (or cry)

will fix just about anything.

CONTENTS

INTRODUCTION

I believe that people are the happiest version of themselves when they are organized. Not happy in a giddy-surge-of-excitement kind of way. Happy in a deeply settled way—the feeling that comes when you've made room for what matters most in your life.

No, I'm not a psychologist (though I'm a big fan of therapy and often recommend it to my clients). I'm a professional organizer, which does mean that I'm trusted to go pretty deep into people's homes and, by default, into their heads as well. While I love it all, it's the latter part that keeps me passionate about my job. The business I founded is called Life in Jeneral, and it's a lifestyle and organizing company that has helped thousands of people simplify and transform their homes into spaces that invite a more joyful way of living.

Our work began in Los Angeles (my home base) and, in the last several years, has taken us across more than fifteen states and into Canada. Our clients are Hollywood celebrities, teachers, military personnel, big families, small families, bachelors, and bachelorettes. They live in every setting, from twenty-five-thousand-square-foot mansions to tiny studio apartments. A client's income level and fame, or the size of their home, could not matter less to me. What matters to me is the intention of the heart. I want to help *anyone* who desires to live more freely and fully by organizing their homes from the inside out. That's why I wrote this book, and why I'm so glad you've picked it up.

My guess is that you, like all of my clients, are in the midst of some kind of transition—moving to a new town and starting a new job, navigating the needs of growing children, bearing through divorce or the death of a loved one—or just navigating through the feeling that a change is needed, even if you can't put your finger on exactly what that might be.

Add the constant transition of life to the frantic speed of twenty-first-century living and you have a giant magnet for the accumulation of belongings. But what's missing is the time and the mental capacity to discern if those things are actually enriching our lives or just distracting us from the bigger picture. It's ironic, isn't it? The more stuff we have, the less time we have to enjoy it. Or each other.

That disconnect breaks my heart because I've personally seen—hundreds of times over—how destructive it can be and how hopeless it can feel to lose touch with the people and the things that give our lives meaning. I never take it for granted that my clients invite me into their homes at some of the most vulnerable times in their lives. It takes an immense amount of courage to let someone into the intimate corners of your home life, to air your dirty laundry—both literally and figuratively. And I'm humbled by that trust every time. It fuels my resolve to see each individual and each family break free from their constant survival mode and step into living with intention. People come to me with tears, shame, and heartbreak, but I always know that my team and I will leave them hopeful, changed, organized, and free to be more fully themselves. Because that is my purpose in this world, and it always has been.

A SOULFUL APPROACH TO ORGANIZING

As far back as I can remember, I've always been a natural streamliner. In elementary school, I convinced one teacher that I should stay back from recess until all the desks were better organized for classroom flow. Looking back, I laugh about what that teacher must've thought of this nine-year-old talking about "maximizing the space to its fullest potential." She must've thought I was crazy, but she was gracious. You've gotta love a good teacher, helping you build your confidence. In middle school, a Saturday-night slumber party at a friend's house turned into an organizing fest with me going deep in my friend's closet, creating *keep, toss,* and *donate* piles on the floor. I know, I'm a real party animal. But while I appreciate the aesthetics of a tidy space, that's not what draws me to organizing. I may not have recognized it in grade school, but my effort to create more efficient spaces is really about how the outcome will make people *feel*. I still remember how excited my friend was at that sleepover when she realized that every single thing in the closet was something she loved.

Having a natural intuition for creating better flow came in quite handy in my early twenties. At that time, I was working as the personal assistant for a professional athlete in LA. My job was to keep all aspects of his daily routine and home life organized. The fact that he moved five times in about as many years might sound like a nightmare for someone in my position, but I saw each move as an opportunity to create increasingly better systems of organization for his home, lifestyle, and priorities. I loved that challenge because I became a firsthand witness to what it looks like when what you own is no longer owning *you* but serving the life you want to lead. The more we simplified and streamlined his living environment, the more at ease and uplifted—the more himself—my employer became. Ultimately, I wanted to make my boss happy, not only with my work but with the rhythm of his daily life. Little did I know that the principles I uncovered in that process would lead to the business I have today.

Perhaps it's because my career in organizing did not begin in a traditional way that my approach with new clients is a little out of the ordinary as well. It's grounded in happiness, and in helping clients figure out what will allow them to live more wholeheartedly in their own homes.

When new clients approach Life in Jeneral, often they have already tried some kind of organizing method themselves or even hired a professional to help overhaul their homes, but it didn't stick. They couldn't maintain the order, and they feel discouraged because of it. Why couldn't they sustain an organized home? Because holistic change requires a holistic approach.

Whenever my team and I begin a new project, before we do anything else, we take time with our clients and ask to hear their stories. We've listened to account after account of how things "just keep piling up" and then life in general (get the company name now?) becomes overwhelming. And while it has always seemed natural to me to seek a fuller picture of someone's life and goals and what makes them tick before we jump into the work needed in their home, most of my new clients are surprised at our efforts to get a deeper understanding of their personal stories. It's not uncommon for me to hear, "No one's ever asked me that before!"

I think one of the biggest misconceptions about organizing is that it can exist in a vacuum—discard, clean, repeat. But in reality, that's totally not the case. Since every facet of our lives is interconnected, our health in one area inevitably affects our health in another. And that's why I've always felt that Life in Jeneral's approach needed to serve both the emotional and physical levels, by (1) seeking to understand a person's values, passions, life goals, and potential emotional hang-ups around possessions that aren't serving the life they want to live; (2) helping them identify and flip the script on those emotional barriers; and (3) creating real *systems* of organization within every space of the home, whereby every item is contained and has a specific and correct home that can be maintained. What we've found along the way is that this effort to encompass more of the whole person, or whole household, in our approach to organizing is what sets up lasting change.

When we ask our clients what their goals are for their homes, we lean in close to catch the answer behind the answer. Because—while it's our bread and butter and an awfully helpful agent of change—achieving an orderly home with a space for everything isn't actually the ultimate goal. It's simply setting the stage for that goal.

I know. It seems counterintuitive for a professional organizer to make that admission. But here's what I've learned from becoming a professional *listener* through this work: no matter the size of a home, the stage of a life, or the makeup of a family, I believe what really matters at the end of the day is connection, love, and purpose. We all long to connect deeply with the ones we love. To experience the lack of striving that comes from being more authentically ourselves. To work and play in meaningful ways. And to hold and acknowledge the sacred moments of life—the laughter, the heartbreak, the breakups and breakthroughs—before our fast-paced world whisks us on to another day. To put it simply, we want to live wholeheartedly . . . starting yesterday. So, why don't we?

CLEARING THE CLUTTERED MIND

Every client I've worked with has a completely unique story with life goals and dreams all his or her own. Yet the reasons they cite for not getting organized or for holding on to objects that are not serving their lives tend to fall into the same six categories:

- I don't have enough time.
- I don't know where to start.
- I don't want to lose the memories.
- I might need it one day.
- I'd feel guilty if I didn't keep this.
- I'd feel lost without my stuff.

Notice a theme? These statements are all *internal* barriers, barriers of the mind and heart: doubts, fears, and anxieties repeated to the point that they become self-limiting mantras.

Whether one rings true for you or you relate to all six, I want to share a truth that can be equal parts encouraging and tough to swallow: the hardest part of ordering your home is *changing your mindset*. Don't worry—I've got you covered on tangible tips, tools, and systems to help you transform your physical space, and I'll share all of that goodness in the pages ahead. But the real work—the *soul work*, I like to say—lies in getting your mind lined up with your heart. Because, as I previously proposed, the human heart already knows what it wants most: the space for deep connection and purposeful living. So, you already have the deep-seated reasons you need to begin the process. It's just time to tap into them.

FLIPPING THE SCRIPT

There is one general fear that often surfaces right away with my clients when I start working with them: their idea of *purging*. By our second conversation (if not the first) they'll nervously ask, "Are you going to make me throw away everything?" Not only am I ready for the question when it comes, I eagerly anticipate it, because my response expresses so much of my core belief around belongings. "No, that's not what we're about," I say. "We're here to focus on what you want to *keep*. Let's rediscover the things you really love in your home."

I am not interested in minimizing for its own sake. My goal is to help my clients simplify so that *every* belonging in their homes either brings them joy or serves a specific, useful function. It's a simple yet profoundly life-changing principle: when you're surrounded by what you love, you can't help but love your surroundings.

When my clients understand the distinction between approaching the process from what they'll *gain* rather than what they'll *lose*, there is an immediate and palpable sense of relief. The task suddenly becomes doable and desirable. Because it is. By starting with "What's most important in your life? What do really you want to keep?" instead of "How much of your stuff can we get rid of?," we've flipped the script.

That's the power of asking the right questions. And that's why for every mental and emotional obstacle to organizing that I cover in the coming chapters, I provide key questions to help you flip the scenario in your mind—to start with a possibility instead of a problem. Using these tools, you'll be able to pivot to a new perspective and to break through these all-too-common barriers on the way to transforming your home.

When it comes to breaking out of mental and emotional ruts worn deep by time and habit, it really helps to have a trustworthy friend in the process. Someone to take you gently by the shoulders and point you toward a new way of thinking about an old challenge. That's why I'm here. We can do this together.

grab a seat
YOUR BREAKTHROUGH BEGINS NOW

Friend, this book is *your* consultation. It's an invitation to sit down on the couch with me, reexamine your own story, and rediscover your big-picture dreams for how you want to experience daily life in your own home.

And perhaps there's never been a better time to do it. As an organizer, I've seen a significant shift in the way people are thinking about their homes. Too often I've seen the heartbreaking effect of a living space that serves only as a frantic transition station for the rest of life or, worse, as an afterthought. But the 2020 pandemic, has—for the first time in a generation—forced us to *be* in our homes more often and for longer periods at a time. That global event required people all over the world to really observe and feel the influence of their home surroundings, and to realize that their homes are meant to be so much more than pass-through points. I think many people experienced a shift during that time, realizing that their homes weren't quite serving them in the most optimal ways, and, more than that, that they *wanted* their homes to be a reflection of what they value most in this life. I heard that a lot, and what I realized is that when people feel stuck within their home spaces—and unsure of how to create change—they often feel like they're stalling out in other places as well. They feel like they don't know where to begin.

This is where I can come in to help. Unpacking the physical and emotional makeup of a home is something I do for a living, and my greatest passion is helping people feel more deeply rooted in who they are and what they want for their lives—and a big part of that comes from realizing the ways in which your home reflects your heart.

In the chapters that follow, I break down each of the most common mental barriers that block the way to establishing an organized and streamlined home. It's not a one-size-fits-all approach; you'll probably see yourself (or people you know) reflected in these pages. The truth is that everyone can experience any number of these mental barriers, and those inevitably prove a hindrance against having the home of your dreams. However, once the emotional clutter is cleared, you'll find practical (and pleasing) solutions for bringing order to the trickiest physical spaces in your home, and the methods to keep it that way.

And here's my favorite part: all along the way, I share the experiences of real clients who have done this *soul* work and seen some incredible breakthroughs in their homes and family lives because of it. Their stories of transformation and growth still get me emotional—in the very best way. I know they will inspire and empower you too.

As we begin this journey together, let this book be (1) your permission slip to ask yourself what you *really* want for your home environment, and (2) the toolbox to help you get there. The way I see it, organizing work is really about caring for yourself and the loved ones in your household in a more holistic way. Your guiding question should always be: How can I shape my home to nurture my heart in this particular season?

It's so tempting to keep one eye on the horizon—and believe me, I get it. We're desperate to mitigate the inevitable changes the future will bring. But that's precious energy spent on something out of your control. By ordering your home around what's best for your life in the present, you are building internal reserves and resiliency for the days ahead. And when we're more resilient, we're not only better equipped to face the challenges that arise, we're able to recognize and embrace more goodness too.

Let's create the space for the life you want to live.

PART 1

soul
work

COMMON EMOTIONAL BARRIERS
AND HOW TO FLIP THE SCRIPT

connection over collection

*WHAT DO YOU REALLY WANT FROM YOUR HOME?
HAS ANYONE EVER ASKED YOU THAT DIRECTLY? OR,
BETTER YET, HAVE YOU EVER HONESTLY
ASKED YOURSELF?*

All too often we're ushered into another phase of our home lives before we're even consciously aware of it, much less actively participating in shaping our surroundings within a changing reality. Maybe we land a new job with a completely different schedule. A new baby arrives or a friend needs a place to land for a while. We need to travel more to check in on an ailing parent. *Life happens*. And sometimes all at once.

It can feel like it takes every ounce of energy and every minute we've got just to keep groceries stocked, work expectations appeased, and the kids alive and well. Our home can take on the pace and frenzy of an emergency room rather than be a place we can depend on for physical and emotional nourishment. We may not be rushing patients into surgery, but we're racing just to find the car keys and to . . . *please* . . . not be late again to school drop-off, the office, that doctor's appointment, and everything else in between. Some days stress levels are high. Resource levels are low. And everyone's in full-on survival mode.

What's truly disheartening to me about this scenario is that many individuals and families I've met have functioned in daily-emergency mode for so long they can't remember—or envision the possibility of—living any other way. But I'm here to tell you that not only is there another way to experience home, it's a joyful, restorative, fulfilling way of living . . . and, most important, it's attainable for everyone.

room to dance
MOVING FROM SURVIVING TO THRIVING

While writing this book, I met a couple who reminded me, in such a poignant way, of why I do what I do. Anna and Greg Delton, a kindhearted and good-humored pair in their thirties with a one-year-old daughter, approached my company for help with their home after finding themselves at an overwhelming intersection of life circumstances they never could have predicted. One year prior they had proudly purchased a new home, had welcomed the arrival of their newborn daughter, Emma, and had been continuing to grow their careers within the entertainment industry. Then, while speeding along in the midst of multiple transitions, all the wheels came off at once. A global pandemic hit, work opportunities came to a screeching standstill, and their beautiful baby girl was diagnosed with a condition that would require special safety precautions in every area of their home.

The effect of it all was paralyzing. By the time Anna reached out to Life in Jeneral, the Deltons had been in their new home for a year, yet moving boxes were still stacked around walls. The belongings they had been able to unpack were stuffed into whatever drawer or cabinet was nearest in the moment or lay in piles on floors and counters. Playtime with their daughter was limited to one room of the house, a space with little furniture and a floor covered in cushions and blankets for her protection. This was supposed to be their new haven—a safe and secure nest to savor their new baby's growth and embrace their new role as parents. Instead, it felt like the space itself was a hazard. They were half moved in and—between learning how to care for their young daughter's emerging needs, coping with complexities caused by the pandemic, and navigating work options in a partially shut-down industry—they were stuck in a cycle that made them feel like they were only half living, all in a house they hadn't been able to truly make a home.

Surrounded by clutter and chaos, Anna and Greg felt too overwhelmed and embarrassed to have any guests over, including their own parents. They dearly wanted their daughter's grandparents to share in the delight of her first milestones. But *where*? There was little uncluttered space in which adults could connect, much less be able to relax with the assurance of their little one's safety. The state of their home had become isolating from the inside out.

When Anna and Greg decided to engage Life in Jeneral's services, it took them months to reach out and even longer to let our team assess the needs of their home. They were nervous, hesitant, and embarrassed. But they *did it*. They knew they wanted more from their home, and they knew they needed help to get unstuck, to get free of an exhausting, defeating daily cycle.

I cannot overstate the significance of simply asking, of just *starting* however you can. It takes tremendous courage to invite others into our mess. Some people wait their entire lives for the "right time" to ask for help. But the Deltons' desire to make their new house a real home, and their urgency to create a safe place for their daughter to thrive, helped them realize that the only "right time" for anyone to begin reclaiming their home life is now.

After the Deltons reached out, my team rallied around them, helping them (1) identify their family's particular needs and goals; (2) purge possessions that didn't support those needs and goals; (3) find the right home for every item and the right system for every space; and, lastly, (4) create areas that fostered connection to each other in a setup that was not only secure for Emma but also inspired creativity and play.

When the process was complete and we took the Deltons on a final walk-through of their transformed home, Anna and Greg were so overcome by relief and joy that they picked up Emma and literally began dancing as a family in the entryway. Witnessing their freedom was so moving that there was no hiding my happy tears. While I strive to be professional, there was no avoiding the emotions that came from the true, pure joy of that shared moment.

As the Deltons began to walk from room to room, reopening every drawer, cabinet, and closet, they kept exclaiming over how the items chosen for each space, and the way they were organized, "just made sense" for their daily lives. I'm not exaggerating . . . *every* drawer and cabinet elicited some kind of huge reaction: "Oh my God!" "You're kidding me!" "This is amazing!" You would have thought you were hearing kids under the tree on Christmas morning instead of middle-aged adults looking inside a neatly organized medicine cabinet or at a bedroom that was now a place of rest instead of a source of stress. Sweet, giddy relief. Gratitude for a fresh start. Their house was finally a home where they could live fully, wholeheartedly, together, in any room on any given day. Moments like these, when a family can dance around together in rooms they could barely walk through before, are why I do what I do.

Life is messy, but it's also so beautiful. And I don't want a single person to miss a single piece of that beauty. Like Anna and Greg, you may not be able to control many of the circumstances life brings your way, but you *can* choose to set up your home in a way that supports and nurtures you and your family. You can create space for who and what is most important to you. And you can put streamlined systems in place to help you sustain it all forever.

It's time to reclaim the power of choice for yourself. You have a say in what you want for your home. And then you get to create it. How incredible is that?

SETTING YOUR INTENTION

So let me ask again: What *do* you want from your home?

If you've never answered that question for yourself, this is the space to do so, right here and right now. Maybe you want to grab a pen and write down what comes to mind. Take your time. Really sit with it. Because finding your heartfelt answer to this question is well worth the intentional pause. In fact, I believe it can change your life.

Please note: I'm not asking about design goals or styling here, though I do believe beautiful aesthetics have an important role to play in loving your home. In this moment, I'm asking what you want your home to *feel* like when you wake up in the morning and step into your daily routine.

What in your home makes you feel happy?

What's most important to you in a home environment?

What kind of lifestyle do you want your living spaces and belongings to support?

What kind of environment would make you feel equipped for the work you need to do each day?

What kind of home would support quality time, both with yourself and with the people you love?

By exploring these kinds of questions, you are setting up guideposts for yourself in how to approach organizing your home—your life's hub—in a way specific to your, and/or your family's, particular needs and goals. Your answers are your own true north, keeping you headed in the right direction, unique to your life circumstances. And it's from this place that you'll be able to successfully navigate the process ahead, determining how your possessions can *support* the kind of daily life you want to lead rather than distract or detract from it.

Keep in mind that these aren't questions you ask yourself just once. I like to think that when it comes to organizing, we're continually engaging with our home spaces; we have the freedom to change over time, and so should they.

STARTING WITH THE "WHY"

Too often, home organization efforts begin (and end) with a sole focus on decluttering, without keeping big-picture values at the forefront. Simply hearing "You have too much stuff" isn't helpful when it comes to long-term change. Sure, you can rid yourself of belongings without determining what you want your life to be centered around. But, frankly, it's an ineffective approach that won't last. Because the *stuff* is not the point. What matters in life are the intangibles—relationships, memories, experiences, a sense of purpose, contributions or service to the world around you, legacy, and, ultimately, how you make people feel. In my view, getting to cherish a messy, wonderful combination of these things is the grand prize of a life well lived.

By assigning our possessions to a supporting role, instead of a starring role, in your life, your true priorities can rise to the top, and everything else will begin to fall into its appropriate place. This approach to living is far more than a theory to me. I believe in it down to my core because it was modeled for me in a deeply personal way throughout my childhood and beyond.

connection over collection
A WAY OF LIFE

For me, having the capacity for meaningful connection with others is by far the most precious benefit of having a streamlined, organized home. There is no other way I'd rather end the day than sitting down for a soulful conversation with someone I care about. Add a glass of wine, a fire pit, and a starry sky and it's my personal heaven. To know others and to be known, to see and appreciate (and maybe chuckle over) the quirky characteristics that make us all different and somehow the same, to love each other well by celebrating the wonderful things and empathizing with the hard and lonely experiences we all share as humans—this is the essence of life to me.

Meaningful connection doesn't require deep conversation in a peaceful outdoor setting, however. (Though I highly recommend it whenever humanly possible.) Connection that adds value to our lives can happen while loading the dishwasher together after dinner. It can be having the space to call your mother for the first time in a while. Cheering on your kid's new scooter skills in the driveway (which, okay, starts with being able to *find* the scooter in your garage). Quietly reading in bed after a long day. An impromptu dance party in the living room. Finally hosting that good buddy from your college days for a weekend. A shared laugh. Even simply keeping calm while helping your kiddo clean up his juice spill.

It can look a million different ways, unique to each individual or family. But whatever it means, living a connected lifestyle *does* require unhurried, non-frantic spaces of time to be present, even if just for a couple of minutes. If your daily life was a story written on a lined page, this kind of space would exist in the margins around the edges of the paper, and even between the lines. A streamlined home, where time isn't continually stolen by lost items, inefficient storage, or clutter and the frustration it brings, has the *margin for moments that matter.*

Growing up, my brother and I got to experience a home environment where connection was the ultimate priority. Sure, our suburban home in Northern California was a bustling one, with two working parents and two kids, who—in between school and other extracurricular activities—played competitive soccer every year, with all the time and travel that entails. But the home atmosphere my parents created still managed to give us generous space for loving connection with them and the many friends, and even new acquaintances, we regularly invited into our home.

While our home was orderly (Mom likes to say I get my organizing genes from her) and comfortable, it was no designer showroom with the latest styles or fashionable furniture. Let's just say the mixed patterns and colors were not on purpose and definitely not of the trendy variety. (Mom, I love you no matter what, but purple floral curtains with a sparkly Sacramento Kings pillow? Seriously?) No doubt about it, I love to create beautiful aesthetics for clients when organizing spaces in their homes, because I know how impactful beauty can be on the way we feel in our surroundings. But I so appreciate my parents' lack of focus on having a magazine cover–worthy home or on acquiring the latest and greatest in material possessions, because it freed up time and energy for all the simple but intentional family moments that turned into wonderful family memories. Whether we were playing soccer, grilling in the backyard and chatting, or spontaneously hosting friends, our home always felt warm and welcoming.

I'm sure my parents made plenty of sacrifices behind the scenes that allowed for this flexibility in our daily family lives, but we kids were never made to feel it. Dad woke up at 4 a.m. to meet his job requirements yet still showed up in his favorite place, our kitchen, most evenings, to cook dinner for all of us. With a white dish towel slung over his shoulder, he was always ready to ask how the day *really* was. When my brother and I were little, these conversations happened around the dinner table. In my teen years, I would pull up a barstool at the kitchen island while Dad whipped up something flavorful and comforting, drawing from his and Mom's Cajun roots. No perfunctory "I'm fine" responses were sufficient. Dad was interested in the state of my heart. When he asked "How are you doing?" he really wanted to know. It was a judgment-free zone, so safe and comforting that even in my awkward teen years, when I was feeling embarrassed by early "boy troubles," I could and did tell him anything and everything. In my college years, these precious moments of connection and conversation spilled into the backyard over glasses of wine on evenings I was home. No matter what was going on in either of our lives, Dad joyfully and intentionally gave me his time and the incredible gift of listening and being present. He consistently created space for meaningful connection—the opportunity to be known. And perhaps nothing has shaped my life more profoundly than that.

It's why "How are you feeling?" is one of the first questions—and always the last question—I ask my clients. I'm not interested in how my company can tidy up your home. I want to know how you're *really* doing, what kind of lifestyle would bring you joy, and how we can transform your home environment to get you there. It's why I can't help but cry when families like the Deltons—who simply wanted to create a loving, life-giving experience of home for their little one—are finally set up and empowered to do so. And it's why I'm so passionate about helping others clear the physical and emotional clutter from their lives so that they can *live* them. Connection over collection. Always.

We've probably all heard that old saying *You can't take it with you when you go* about our material possessions and what we leave behind when passing from this life. I come back to that principle with my clients when we're working through clutter that is holding them back from the life they want but that they still can't seem to let go of. It helps when we shift the focus and ask, "What *can* we leave behind that truly lasts?"

From Dad's example, I've seen that being intentional with the way you show care and give your presence to others is the way to create a true, lasting legacy. How you inspire people, how you make them *feel*—that's what continues to offer light and warmth long after you're gone.

My dad passed away two years after I graduated from college. And there literally isn't a single day, not one, that I don't miss him. But I think I finally understand that expression about a personality being *larger than life* because Dad's presence—his way of connecting with and loving people—was and is transcendent. It's because of the way he *lived* that I do what I do. It's my why. I don't organize and simplify homes to create pretty places for people to live. I help people create a nurturing space around them and their families so that they can focus on living more fully and openly from their hearts like Dad did. Because that's where happiness finds *you*, not the other way around.

All these years after Dad's passing, I still get messages from my friends and our family's friends telling me what he meant to them. They tell me how Dad made them feel and about the influence his generosity and willingness to "take the time" had on their lives. My old college buddies still remind me of the times when we would get home at 2 a.m. and Dad—who had made me promise to wake him up when we got in—would jump and make us all steaks in the middle of the night, sometimes staying up to talk with us until the first rays of morning light came through the kitchen windows. Those friends will say, "Who does that?!"—still smiling at how special and valued he made us all feel.

My brother and I may have been my dad's only biological children, but he was a father to a hundred. And probably more. *That* kind of legacy is what we have the power to leave behind if we center our lives around what matters most.

HOW WE THINK ABOUT OUR "THINGS"

When we think about leaving a legacy, many people fixate on physical objects. Makes sense, right? Physical objects can show an accomplishment, remind you of a wonderful time shared with loved ones, and can reinforce a belief in yourself. So it's significant to note that how we generally think about and consider our physical belongings matters more than you might imagine. Because inanimate objects aren't living or breathing, we tend to take it for granted that they have some sort of a neutral presence in our homes: neither good nor bad, just *there*. But the very fact that every object—no matter how small—takes up space means that each one has an effect on its surroundings. Every object must be moved and moved around, be used or not used, be enjoyed, be worried about, or be ignored. Even things you may forget about for months or years at a time—items stuffed up in the top of a guest closet or down in the far reaches of the basement—use up energy. Maybe that energy simply takes the form of a nagging thought periodically cycling through your brain, reminding you that your good intentions for those belongings continue to go unfulfilled. No matter how slight their intrusion on your space and consciousness, those stashed and semiforgotten items are still stealing, bit by bit, from your life's energy. Energy that could be used or saved for something else important to you. Something productive, meaningful, or joyful. After all, isn't our energy one of our most precious resources?

I'd like to propose that the objects in our homes fall, for the most part, into two categories: *life-giving things* and *life-taking things.*

Life-giving things are belongings you either *love, use, or need.* They serve to make life doable and/or delightful. An item you *love* should make you feel good every time you see it or come in contact with it (e.g., the beautiful vase that inspires you to bring in fresh flowers, the framed photo or piece of art that always lifts your spirit, or the funny little pillow your grandmother made that you hug sometimes just to feel her presence). Items you *use* or *need* are things that either have a specific, utilitarian function in your regular rhythm of living (e.g., a coffeepot, curling iron, or toothbrush) or are essential to your lifestyle, health, and wellness (e.g., a bicycle, musical instrument, or set of watercolors). While they aren't always the same thing, I put the categories *use* and *need* together because if an item is something you *need* to maintain the lifestyle you want, you will *use* it at least semiregularly. Simply put, life-giving things are things worth keeping. And it's important to note that life-giving (and -taking) items will be different for every person depending on individual daily routines, needs, goals, and dreams. I can't overemphasize how crucial it is to avoid comparing yourself to others when determining whether an object does or doesn't serve your life. This is your home and your story—you get to decide what's right for you.

Life-taking things are possessions that accumulate to the point of stealing our time, our money, our sanity, our energy, and our freedom to say yes to things. As the opposite of life-giving, they are things that we *don't* truly love, use, or need. In a word, they are *clutter*. If you look beyond the surface, you'll see that clutter is a physical symptom of a mental or emotional issue. Clutter is made up of the objects we tend to collect when living and making decisions out of fear, insecurity, or uncertainty.

But fear doesn't get to drive. Not on the road trip of this one precious life, and not on the journey to building a home life that nurtures you and your family. The clutter we see in our homes, as you'll see in the next few chapters, often reflects what we're feeling inside: the ways in which we're *afraid* to change.

By holding on to items we don't love, use, or need, we are—often subconsciously—attempting to hang on to the past or to control the future. But what we're actually doing is building barriers that block us from living fully in the present and limit our ability to connect with others and our own authentic, internal voices.

In the next six chapters, we'll work through some of the most common mental and emotional barriers to organizing and creating life-giving, sustainable structure within your home. You may find that you identify with more than one of these self-imposed obstacles, or even that you identify with all six. As we walk through these mindsets together, I want to encourage you to take your time in reflecting not only on each roadblock but also on your responses to the questions you just answered about what you really want for your home. It could be that some of these emotional sticking points are key players in keeping you from your home goals and dreams. Be honest with yourself about what you discover in your own inner dialogue. There's nothing to lose here . . . and so much to gain.

I won't do you the disservice of sugarcoating the soul work it takes to go beyond the symptoms of clutter to figuring out why it has gotten out of hand or why we haven't dealt with it. It will require deep digging, not only into the contents of your home but also into the emotional and physical habits that haven't served you in the past. But if you have the courage for honest self-reflection and the willingness to remain open to the process, you already have everything you need for the task at hand. No, it won't be easy—but the payoff is going to be *so* incredibly worth it.

i don't have
enough time

TURN AN "ENEMY" OF ORGANIZATION INTO
AN ALLY FOR LIVING WITH INTENTION.

If you only looked at Nicole's life *outside* of her chic Hollywood townhouse, it appeared she had made it to the top of what life had to offer. When I met her, Nicole, an extremely talented stylist in her late forties, had been working her tush off in a fast-paced industry for more than two decades. It had paid off, and her styling prowess was sought after by celebrities across the country.

But if you were to step *inside* the entryway of Nicole's home, you would have immediately known something wasn't right. Her hallway and floors were the victims of a job that required almost constant travel, sometimes at a moment's notice. Mounds of leftover product and clothing from endless photo shoots for clients, stacks of paperwork and magazines, and piles of odds and ends from suitcases that had been dumped out only to be hastily repacked made little space for walking between rooms or finding a chair to sit down on. But Nicole was barely home long enough between gigs to sit down anyway. It wasn't that she didn't need a break; she was desperately exhausted and stressed in every way. Yet even though her business was flourishing and she had money in the bank, she wouldn't turn down a client no matter how last-minute his or her call. She said yes to everything and everyone. Except herself.

The heartbreaking part is that amid all the demands for her time and talent, Nicole felt incredibly lonely. She wanted to find a significant other, but felt she didn't have time to date. She loved to host, but hadn't had guests over to her home in more than ten years. After all, the guest room was cluttered to the point of being unusable, as was much of the rest of the townhouse, and Nicole was too ashamed to invite anyone into the mess (including me, at least at first).

Who knows how much longer she would have kept up this maddening pace and lifestyle if her body and mind hadn't called it quits when they did. On one of hundreds of flights back home to Los Angeles after a job, Nicole had a panic attack. She was overcome by the dread of returning home to the point that she could hardly breathe. Such was the negative and guilt-laden energy she felt returning to the place that should have been her haven of comfort and rest. That scary incident on the plane was Nicole's tipping point and perhaps her saving grace. Realizing that she could not continue to go on this way, she called Life in Jeneral the next day.

After talking with Nicole and hearing the urgency in her story, I worked to schedule a site visit to her home as soon as possible to get a full picture of the kind of support she needed. But even though she was highly anxious to change the environment of her home (and I checked in with her weekly), it was six more months before she would summon the courage and overcome her embarrassment enough to let me in her door.

Once she did, our work began. And while my team and I helped Nicole address her mountains of physical clutter, she also began to dig out from under the emotional baggage that had so long buried her personal desires. Underneath her inability to set boundaries or turn down a client to preserve needed personal time, Nicole found fear. Fear that if she let up for one moment, disappointed one client, or took one break, everything she had built would fall apart. Even with the sizable success she had achieved, her lack of confidence in her own value and contributions confined her to a constant state of striving. No achievement would be good enough to relieve the fear of failure or rejection. The wildly out-of-control clutter in her home had become an apt reflection of her inner life, the one she had been keeping under wraps—just like her home—until she couldn't any longer.

By making the first call to our office, by letting me in the door, by working through the full process with my team to simplify and restore her home to a place of peace and respite, Nicole had *finally* prioritized herself. She chose to assign value to her personal time, space, and well-being. That courageous act of trust resulted in a level of transformation that is something I still marvel at today. And I'm not talking about her townhouse, though that transformation was pretty amazing too.

In one way or another, Nicole is each of us. You may not be jet-setting on a panic-attack level for your job or be unable to walk down your hallway due to clutter, but my guess is that you, like me and like each one of my clients, often feel stretched thin. How and when are we supposed to get it all done?

HOW WE THINK ABOUT TIME

"I just don't have enough time." I'll bet that phrase feels familiar to you. After all, lack of time is the most common obstacle I hear clients talk about to explain why they feel unable to tackle organizing their homes in a sustainable manner. I can't help but sympathize. I'm definitely not immune to the feeling that "there just aren't enough hours in the day." In fact, I feel that way more often than I'd like to admit. But I have to catch myself when I'm functioning out of a not-enough-time mentality because, at its core, it's problematic thinking.

Time itself hasn't changed. It is what it is. There aren't fewer hours in a day than there were before. There are still twenty-four, and health professionals still agree that about one-third of those should be spent in sleep. So, what *has* changed? Well, for one thing: technology and our relationship to it. While the digital age was supposed to make our lives easier—shout out to online grocery orders and curbside pickup!—it has also raised our expectations of what can or should be accomplished in a day's time to an unrealistic level. In other words, because we technically *can* do more and do it faster, we assume we *should* be doing more, in general.

Busyness has practically become a social status symbol, a badge of honor. Overcommitment is confused for engagement. Most of us compare our overbooked calendars and levels of exhaustion, yet we often don't use all of our paid time off at work. It's a depleting way to live. Yet it's the cultural current we find ourselves caught up in today. And it's taking a toll, adding to what social researchers like Brené Brown call "a culture of scarcity." Whether consciously or subconsciously, many of us are functioning out of a common, underlying belief that there just aren't *enough* internal or external resources to thrive, particularly the resource of time.

Does the following dynamic sound familiar? You wake up in the morning feeling like you didn't get enough rest, only to go to bed that night feeling like you didn't get enough done. We start and end every day with a sense of lack, a mindset of scarcity.

If one of your repeated arguments with life is that there's not enough time to do what's needed, much less wanted, you're not alone. For many of the individuals I work with, that's the broken record that has been playing on an endless loop for much of their adult lives. But just like my clients have done, you can choose to play a new track. You can create a new relationship with time by starting with a different perspective.

flip the script
WHAT DO YOU WANT TO HAVE TIME FOR?

Instead of spending energy wishing for more time, what if you began asking yourself *"What do I want to have time for?"* Then the focus wouldn't be on the impossible (creating more hours in a day), it would be on identifying what's important to you right now, something you really want or need in this particular season. And that's not only achievable, it's a game changer.

Resist the temptation to look anywhere but inward—not to other families or to cultural norms—as you ask yourself the question. What is one thing you wish you had the capacity for right now? What is something you want to pursue or do differently in this season that would bring you more joy, peace, relief, rest, fun, or connection?

Is it to cook more healthy meals at home and eat together as family? Is it to cook less and order in more so you can slow down and focus on conversation (or maybe retreat to your room with a good book)? Do you want to schedule a monthly phone call with a close friend you miss, the one that always lifts your spirit with humor and empathy? Begin the first online course for the degree you've always wanted? Take a walk every evening to release the day? Take a hot soak in the tub with no one rushing you? Say yes to more spontaneous family bike rides or outings?

For me, when I pause to think about what I want time for, more and more often the answer is "disconnecting from technology and devices and connecting with someone I love." While I'm deeply passionate about my work, running a business can cause me to feel like I'm always *on call*, always a text or email away from needing to plug back into work mode, no matter the time of day or night. I live close to some wonderful trails, and my fiancé often asks me to hike with him. A simple way to make time for what I want in this season is to say "yes" next time he asks, and then to leave my phone safely at home so I can be fully present for every step.

What you want time for right now might be something small or simple. My client, Nicole, just wanted to be able to have someone over for dinner, to have a guest room ready for that friend that stayed over late for good wine and conversation. It wasn't a dramatic ask, but the simple pleasure of hosting a friend was one of the bright lights at the end of her tunnel. For Nicole, the rewards of that kind of connection were worth *making* the time for.

A small delight can bring a great amount of joy and restoration, and once your default routine has been shifted—however slightly—to make space for this new ritual, it will create an opening for more creativity and inspiration, making it easier to try another small life-giving change or addition. And suddenly you'll find that the choices and changes are becoming bigger, moving you toward the home environment and lifestyle goals you identified for yourself in chapter 1.

As counterintuitive as it may seem, acknowledging that time is finite can be incredibly liberating. When we accept the reality of time as limited, we understand that we must truly prioritize our days or we will spend our lives missing the things that make it rich with depth, texture, meaning, and levity—the (often simple) things that make life *good*. The fact that our days, hours, and minutes are numbered is the very thing that makes them precious. And when we structure our routines—and our homes—out of that perspective, we're able to make choices with our time that better support our values and goals.

Reprioritizing the actions to which we give our time will require setting real boundaries and holding to them. It will mean letting go of certain activities that don't make the cut. It will mean gently but firmly saying *no* to invitations or requests that no longer serve the ultimate goals of your household. But it also will mean that when you say *yes* to something, you can say it with your whole heart. And I can't think of a truer way to honor the time we've been given.

DISORGANIZATION, A MASTER THIEF

So what does all of this have to do with making time to organize your home? It's a pretty straightforward connection: if you *make* the time to simplify and streamline your home, you will *have* the time to do the things you really want to do.

When all of your well-used and loved belongings have proper homes and are consistently where they need to be, you'll be spending a lot less time looking for lost items, tidying, restacking, moving clutter from place to place, and maintaining items that are somewhere they shouldn't be. Ironically, while we're constantly wishing for "more time," we're often oblivious to what is stealing the time we do have. And disorganization is one of the trickiest thieves of all.

According to a 2017 survey by Pixie Technology, Inc., Americans spend 2.5 days a year just looking for misplaced items.[1] That's about six months of an average American's lifespan. Half a year of our lives spent stressed, rushed, annoyed, panicked, and running late all because an item—usually something as simple as our keys, our phone, the TV remote, our glasses, or a pair of shoes—isn't where it needs to be when we need it.

And that's just the most visible tip of the iceberg. What may be less obvious, but no less significant, are the ways chaos and clutter negatively impact your time by draining other precious personal resources. When your home is disorganized, every transition throughout the day can feel more difficult. Something as seemingly insignificant as searching for your keys in the morning can set off a chain of events that you'll probably never trace back to the starting point. It's the classic snowball effect. You can't find your keys and now you're running late, so you snap at your kids for taking too long to get ready for school, which leads to a fight with your partner, which leads to you feeling "off" in an important meeting at the office. The meeting doesn't go well and your stress level increases, which affects how you feel going into the rest of your workday. You're still in a funk by the time you pick up the kids from school and head home to start all over, but the house is still a mess, your partner is still in a bad mood from your fight, and you still don't have a place to put your keys so that you remember them next time.

But what if the keys had been in their proper place and you never had to search for them to begin with? How many layers of negativity, mental and physical exhaustion, and strain on relationships could've been avoided by such a simple difference at the start of the day?

---

1 Pixie Technology, Inc., "Lost and Found: The Average American Spends 2.5 Days Each Year Looking for Lost Items Collectively Costing U.S. Households $2.7 Billion Annually in Replacement Costs," *PR Newswire*, May 2, 2017, https://www.prnewswire.com/news-releases/lost-and-found-the-average-american-spends-25-days-each-year-looking-for-lost-items-collectively-costing-us-households-27-billion-annually-in-replacement-costs-300449305.html.

DIGITAL CLUTTER AND THE TRAP
OF THE ENDLESS NEWS FEED

In the organizing world, we talk about *taking inventory* of the contents of your home. I think it's equally important to take inventory on how we spend our time. Have you ever tracked where the minutes go throughout your average weekday? You might be surprised at what you find.

But maybe you already know what the other chief time-stealer is for the average person. After all, we've even given it its own time-related term: *screen time.*

In a TED Talk that's been viewed close to four million times, the psychologist Adam Alter shares his research on the effect of screens and technology on our lives.[2] He studied how the average twenty-four-hour day has changed over a decade, and what he found was that the amount of time we spend on most activities hasn't changed much. Most people still sleep roughly around seven to eight hours a day and still work around eight to nine hours a day. And the average working person still spends about three hours a day in what Alter calls "survival activities" (e.g., eating, bathing, and caring for children). That leaves a few hours of flexible or discretionary time. And *that* is where Alter found a dramatic difference in how we spend our time now. He discovered that, on average, the amount of discretionary time most people spend on activities that do *not* include staring at a screen is about half an hour.[3]

Friend, did you catch that? Half. An. Hour. After screen time has taken its due, that's the amount of flexible time the average person has to cram in

---

2 Adam Alter, "Why Screens Don't Make Us Happy," filmed July 2017 in Toronto, Canada, TED video, 9:22, https://www.ted.com/talks/adam_alter_why_our_screens_make_us_less_happy.
3 Kaitlin Luna and Adam Alter, "The Dark Side of Screen Time," May 2019, in *Speaking of Psychology*, produced by the American Psychological Association, podcast audio, https://www.apa.org/research/action/speaking-of-psychology/screen-time.

personal enrichment, connective time with loved ones, hobbies, exercise, or self-reflection. Before DVRs or Netflix, watching your favorite TV program had a start and a stop time. But streaming has made access to digital content limitless. We no longer have what Alter calls "stopping cues" at the end of a program. As a result, endless news cycles, social media feeds, and mindless scrolling are replacing some of the most restorative parts of our days. They're stealing the moments we could have used to do something that would energize our spirits, reignite our hearts, strengthen our bodies, remind us of our shared humanity, or provide needed comfort to ourselves or others.

This loss of connection and what it can mean for our collective resilience in the days ahead is deeply disheartening to me. But it also drives me to continually reexamine my own priorities like my life depends on it because, in many ways, it does. And it fires me up to challenge and encourage you to do the same. Small shifts—as small as putting your phone on silent and out of sight during dinner—can move us toward treating time as the gift it is and home as a sacred space to enjoy it.

time is a gift
HOW WE SPEND IT IS A CHOICE

Gratitude is the not-so-secret ingredient needed for embracing a new perspective. Acknowledging time for what it is and giving thanks for the moments we've been given sets us up to make better choices for how we spend our days. And *having a choice* is a gift in itself.

Please know that I'm not suggesting that everyone has the same amount of flexible time. Because, of course, that simply isn't the case. Parents of young children, and caregivers of any kind, along with those whose vocations or life circumstances require working through the night hours, are time-juggling heroes. But even taking care of the undeniable responsibilities unique to each of our lives is, in essence, a choice. We each have the opportunity to fill our lives with the things that deserve to be there.

And prioritizing the organization of your home creates more capacity to do just that. Here's the catch, though: you must choose to believe in the value of your own time in order to make that leap. I'll take it a step further: you have to be willing to prioritize *yourself*. If you're a giving person, and I'll bet you are, I know that last statement probably triggered a twinge of guilt. After all, how can we put ourselves first when there are others we are responsible for and so many things on our to-do lists that we "should" be taking care of?

But here's another way to think about it: What would you do if you knew that investing in your own well-being would benefit everyone you came in contact with? Okay, pause for a minute to find your answer. Now, whatever you just answered, do that. Because here's the reality: the more whole, happy, rested, and restored you are, the more you'll have to give to those around you.

BREAKTHROUGH BELIEFS

The *very day* my team finished our work in Nicole's home, she invited a friend over for dinner and to spend the night in her guest room. She had denied herself the joy of hosting for more than ten years and wasn't about to wait a minute longer. While Nicole's business continues to thrive, she has scaled back on the number of jobs she's willing to take on and scaled up on time for herself. Her confidence has grown, she's physically healthier than she's been in years, and she's dating again. But what I love most about Nicole's story is that once she decided to prioritize herself and embrace the gift of her whole life—not just her career—the joy she found began to overflow on to other people, people she could finally enjoy and care for in the warmth and comfort of her own well-loved home.

If you've longed to create a more peaceful and fulfilling home life, free of physical and mental clutter, but you've never taken action because you "just don't have the time," let Nicole's transformation inspire you to seize the day—to take hold of a new belief and make a new declaration:

> I know I'll have the time for what I really want to do if I make the time to get organized now. Time is a gift, and I choose to prioritize the home that nurtures me so that I can be the best version of myself—for my own well-being, the ones I love, and the world around me.

As you prepare to move into the practical steps for organizing your home I've laid out in part II, you may find it helpful to come back to this declaration throughout the process. It's here when you need to get back into the right headspace. Say it when you're struggling to stay committed, when you want to jump ship midway through because it's still hard to "find the time." It took years to form your old belief about time; it will take repetition (and some rewarding results) to form a new one.

MAKE THE TIME, MAKE A PLAN

You may need a full, uninterrupted week to simplify and streamline your home. Or you may need a full year, working from room to room, addressing a new space each month. There are a couple of factors at play here, the first being emotions. Organizing can be emotionally exhausting! I've seen so many clients who are ready to part ways with stuff, but then feel surges of guilt over letting go of that never-worn piece of jewelry gifted to them five years back, or the pair of jeans they were hoping to fit into a year ago. The emotions behind this stage can't be understated.

The second factor is time. Just as anyone's amount of flexible time is unique to their life circumstances, so too is the state of anyone's home when they begin the organizing process. It's not the size of a home that will dictate how long the organizing process takes, it's the amount of inventory. In chapter 8, we'll help you determine an approach for your own living spaces and family situation. You'll be able to make a plan for how you'll prioritize the time to get it done. A real plan—the kind you map out on the calendar and talk about with a trusted friend or family member who will encourage you and hold you accountable.

I know it can be tough to hear, but "waiting for a free weekend" is not a plan. It's a wish at best, but not a plan based on reality. The truth is, if you haven't already locked in on the value of a streamlined home, then even if you find yourself with a gloriously free weekend, you're unlikely to spend it on organizing in a sustainable manner. Let's give up the postponing-until-a-better-time tactic. In truth, that's really planning for it never to happen. Sharpie that shit into your calendar. You owe it to yourself.

But here's the best news: if you commit to organizing your home the right way (following the correct steps mapped out in the pages ahead), the systems you'll build can last a lifetime. Even when the seasons in your life change, your family looks different, or you move into a new home, you'll have the knowledge you need, and the systems in place to sustain it all. You'll ask the right questions, purchase and bring things into your home differently, and make better decisions about your belongings. Yes, organizing your home is an investment of time, but it's an investment with lifelong returns. And the only regret I ever hear from clients is that they wish they'd done it sooner.

When every item in your home has a proper home, you'll spend less time searching for misplaced things and more time doing what you need and want to do.

i don't know
where to start

ACHIEVE BIG VICTORIES IN ORGANIZING,
BEGINNING WITH BITE-SIZE WINS.

When I met Gayle, she was so overwhelmed by the need to purge, organize, and box up her family's home of twenty-five years that even thinking about beginning the task rendered her completely paralyzed. "I don't know how to do this," she confided to me through tears. "I don't even know where to start."

As the spouse of a business owner whose job required constant travel, Gayle's home had been an anchor for her, their kids, and, more recently, their grandchildren. It was not only her haven, headquarters, and place for hosting, it was truly an extension of herself—her means of providing consistent care for her loved ones, particularly her young granddaughter with special needs. But now the company's headquarters was being strategically relocated across the country and that meant Gayle and her husband, Carl, were relocating too.

When she reached out to Life in Jeneral, Gayle's request seemed fairly straightforward: we were coming in to help her organize their belongings and create storage systems before boxing it all. That way when everything was unpacked in their new home two thousand miles away, the process of setting up her household in an orderly manner would be relatively simple.

It was a great plan. But not only was the move itself deeply emotional for Gayle, the collection of physical stuff, accumulated over a quarter century of living and three generations of family members coming and going, was quite deep too. When I arrived at her home, she was sitting at the kitchen table crying. Hard. She knew that if she didn't get a handle on simplifying their belongings, the move-in would be even more stressful than it already felt. But that pressure and the size of the task at hand had her frozen to that kitchen chair.

failure to launch
WHAT'S BEHIND THE PROCRASTINATION?

It doesn't take a move across the country (or anywhere at all) to become paralyzed by the idea of organizing a home top to bottom, or by any sizable task for that matter. While everyone has their own rationale for putting things off, there are two main reasons why most of us procrastinate:

1. We despise being uncomfortable. We're afraid of the unpleasantness of a challenging task, so we avoid it. This is a double-edged sword because while we're busy dodging the discomfort of a task that would make our lives better, we're piling up (in some cases years' worth of) dread and guilt for not doing what we know is best. Ironically, we would experience so much more relief by just getting started on this work that has become larger than life in our minds.

2. Perfectionism. We're terrified of failure. We'd rather not do something at all than plunge in without feeling like we know how to do it, or do it well. Our unrealistic expectations of ourselves become our own trap. Perhaps there's nothing as self-limiting as not giving ourselves the grace to jump in and learn along the way.

Gayle had both of these dynamics at play. And her discomfort around the physical task was made even more acute because of the grief she was experiencing in leaving the home that symbolized stability and comfort for her. I knew that this loving matriarch felt like a forlorn queen losing her beloved castle. The one domain that had been in her charge for so many years felt completely out of control. The idea of starting over, of reestablishing her household, was overwhelming. She didn't want to "get it wrong."

As I sat at the kitchen table with Gayle and listened to her pour out her anxiety, fear, and exhaustion, I knew she needed a victory and quickly. We went over the plan I had put together for her home and the move. And as Gayle dried her eyes, I told her, "I know everything seems larger than life right now, so let's start with something small." And then I asked the oh-so-simple, yet surprisingly effective question for getting my clients moving: "What is one small thing you can do right now that doesn't feel overwhelming?"

LITTLE WINS, BIG MOMENTUM

Usually, that "small thing" or starting point is literally a small space (think cabinet or drawer) in the home. For Gayle, I suggested the *joy drawer* in the center of her kitchen. What is a joy drawer? It's what I've named the command-center drawer of a home. It's what a *catch-all* or *junk drawer* becomes when it's no longer holding a jumble of random odds and ends, but instead keeping the essentials for your daily comings and goings tidy and easily accessible, making those daily transitions more joyful. (See chapter 16 for more on organizing a joy drawer.) Not only does the small size of the joy-drawer space make it feel more doable, but I knew that the miscellaneous contents of a catch-all drawer aren't typically very emotionally charged, which was helpful for Gayle in that moment.

The process was simple. We took everything out of the drawer, laid each item on the kitchen counter, and then sorted like things together. Then, as she lifted each object, I asked her very simple questions: Do you use that? How often? Is there a better home for it than this prime-real-estate spot?

We flew through the drawer's contents.

Old local restaurant menus? A new city meant new restaurants, and menus were all online now anyway. Tossed.

Thirteen pens? We threw out the six that didn't work and kept her and Carl's two favorite pens in the drawer. She'd take the rest to the office.

Checkbook? (Yep, she still used one.) The kitchen was where she paid bills. Kept.

Lip balm? She never liked that brand anyway. Tossed.

Five notebooks? They'd been used and she didn't have a purpose for them. Donate pile.

Keys? Kept.

Hammer? Even Gayle had to laugh at this one. She'd never used this hammer
   in the many years it had found residence in this prime spot, yet it took up a
   quarter of the drawer. It went to the garage, ten feet away.

With every decision she made on her joy-drawer inventory, Gayle's posture
got a little straighter and her eyes got a little clearer. This task was doable.
It was even, she discovered, a little exciting. She felt empowered by making
small but definitive decisions. By the time the drawer's contents were simplified, organized into a tray, and ready to be boxed up for a similar drawer
in her new home, Gayle was looking around for the next small thing to
tackle. High fives all around. Next stop? The spice cabinet.

flip the script
START SMALL

If Gayle's initial breakthrough in organizing her home seems simplistic,
that's because it was. On purpose. It's easy to underestimate a small win,
but if you trace them back, most big victories are made out of a collection of small ones. It's tough to get our minds and bodies moving in the
right direction from a standstill, especially when we've been sidelined by
overwhelming circumstances and self-doubt. But if we can toss ourselves
a softball, something easy to hit out of the park, we'll gain momentum.
When you feel daunted and paralyzed by your own, don't let it stall you
out. Instead, just as I asked Gayle, ask yourself: *"What is one small thing
I can do right now that doesn't feel overwhelming?"* Tackle that jewelry tray
on top of the dresser or the little cabinet under the kitchen sink, and you'll
be ready and able to move toward the next task, powered by a little bit

more confidence and a burst of good energy, thanks to the way our brains work.

When we experience any success, no matter the size, our brain rewards us by releasing dopamine, a feel-good hormone linked to motivation. And the more small victories you achieve in a row, the more constant your supply of dopamine. Put simply, small wins are addictive in the very best way. Even as a professional organizer, doing this work day in and day out, I still feel that amazing lift whenever I'm able to bring order and beauty to a previously chaotic space. It gets me every time, boosting my excitement and creativity for the next project.

It's honestly hard to describe the amazing feeling you'll experience from your own organizing wins. Truly, it will feel so *good* to step back and look at a space that is now free of clutter, with everything you need beautifully contained and at the ready, all because of your efforts. You just have to experience it to believe how exhilarating it can be.

But there's no way around the fact that working through a mess is, well, messy. I say it all the time: it gets worse before it gets better. When you're working through the process of thoroughly organizing your home, laying out every object in a space to be sorted in piles and all the hidden clutter is now out in the open, it can feel chaotic, overwhelming, and discouraging. Here you are taking the time out of your busy schedule to do this work. You're interrupting your routine and putting in the effort. All you want is a peaceful, efficient space, yet it currently looks more like a disaster than ever. When you come to this place in the process, if you're not buoyed by the gratification of some smaller yet satisfying successes, proof that it's doable and worth it, you'll give up before the magic happens.

That's why, when it comes to organizing your home, I always recommend starting with spaces that are literally small in size with a limited amount of inventory and fewer complex decisions to be made.

Start with a joy drawer, medicine cabinet, bathroom vanity, cleaning-supply closet, or spice cabinet. Save areas heavy with paperwork, photos, or memorabilia for last. Believe me, you never want to start your organizing journey with those kinds of items. I can't tell you how many times I've seen a client derail their own progress by hitting these more mentally draining or emotionally charged areas too early on. Trust the process. Start small and build up. Just like Gayle did.

That's not to say that the kitchen table was the last of Gayle's purging, organizing, and moving tears—and that was with a team of professionals working alongside her. Her overarching victory with organizing and relocating her household was hard-won. The joy drawer wasn't the only bite-size breakthrough needed, it was simply the first. But Gayle's early successes fueled her forward momentum, and I watched her grow as a person in the process. It was no surprise that when we got to the crux of it all—her piles and piles of paperwork—she had another momentary stall-out. I vividly remember Gayle holding an old bill over the shredder with her hand literally shaking, just willing herself to let go of a false sense of security. But with encouragement from my team, she stuck to the process and the plan we had mapped out together.

PROGRESS OVER PERFECTION

Most people do want an orderly home with space to breathe. They *want* to be rid of the clutter. They *want* the freedom to focus on their priorities. So what's the holdup? Sometimes part of the paralysis of perfectionism is a lack of confidence stemming from a lack of know-how.

Maybe, like lots of my clients, you've wondered if you're missing some innate organizing ability that should've been imparted at birth, or, at the very least, taught in grade school. But here's the truth: most people I know are not "natural organizers." That's why I'm writing this book.

And here's something else: even if you could take ten of the best organizers in the world, and give them the same space—let's say the same disorderly kitchen pantry—to organize, all ten people are going to create something different. Sure, they might adhere to the same basic principles, but the ways each of them approaches the space will be unique. You're creating something unique to you and your home. It doesn't need to be "perfect." (What *is* perfect anyway? Nothing real, attainable, or helpful. So, let it go.) It simply needs to serve the life *you* want to lead.

When fear of getting it wrong threatens to stall you out in the organizing process, the key is to just keep moving. Break the current task or space you're on into smaller bites. Find another easy win that you can tackle next.

Believe it or not, by the last day of organizing and packing up her home, Gayle was *throwing* papers gleefully into the designated shred-it pile. I'm not exaggerating. That's how light she had become by the end of the process. It still brings a smile to my face to think about what an overcomer Gayle became through the experience of organizing and moving her home—from allowing herself tears and paralyzing fears to tossing away papers like it was her job.

You will achieve that lightness too. And it gives me so much joy knowing that, as you kick-start your plan with little victories, you will begin to feel a weight, one you may never have been fully aware was on your shoulders, begin to lift. It might come gradually, but it will come. You just need to *start,* and start small.

i don't want to lose the memories

LET SENTIMENTAL OBJECTS POINT YOU TO
THE INTANGIBLE VALUE WITHIN.

Natalie was only thirty-five when her husband, John, suddenly passed away. When she called Life in Jeneral, more than a year after his death, Natalie was still struggling to imagine a life without her best friend and husband. She knew she needed to move forward, to create her own meaningful life and future. She even felt like it might be time to launch her long-held dream of running her own photography business out of her home. It's what she wanted and what John had wanted for her. But she still felt lost and unsure of how to reshape her home and her life without John in it.

When I met Natalie for our first walk-through of her home, I could feel her anxiety about the prospect of organizing her belongings, of making changes in the living spaces she and John had shared for more than ten years. The fear came to a head when we reached the spare room in her home. Over the past eighteen months, Natalie had begun to bring John's things—clothes, toiletries, and memorabilia—that she didn't know what to do with into this room. And now it was full. As she opened the door to show me, I could tangibly feel and see a wave of sadness and grief wash over her. And I could feel something else too: dread. Dread stemming from the heaviness of knowing decisions needed to be made about these belongings, but feeling powerless to make them.

An impressive number of men's jackets and blazers was taking up a significant portion of the room. More than thirty in total. When I asked Natalie about them, she began to walk me through the memories attached to each one: this jacket was the one he wore on their first date. That suit coat was the one he wore in their wedding. This was the blazer he wore to dinner on their tenth anniversary, when he'd surprised her with a getaway to a city she'd always wanted to visit.

Natalie cried as she shared story after story. And I cried with her. I understood what it feels like when treasured memories with your loved one become even more sacred because you know there will not be any new ones to be made. How could she let these tactile garments go when they seemed so full of the person she could no longer put her arms around?

I sat and listened to Natalie's sweet remembrances of John and their life together and dreams for the future in that spare room for a long time. I knew that what she really wanted to keep close weren't thirty jackets in a spare room that made her sad to enter. She wanted to keep the essence of John himself and the precious memories with him that those coats symbolized.

But what if, I gently suggested, she could keep those symbols in another form—one that freed up both physical and emotional space for her present and future life to grow?

After encouraging Natalie to select three of John's jackets to keep—the three she cherished most—I arranged for the rest of the jackets to be professionally photographed in her home and printed into a beautiful keepsake book. With every photograph taken, I could feel Natalie's fear subside bit by bit and her relief begin to grow. That book became her tangible assurance that while she would gain back the physical space of the room, she wouldn't lose the memories those jackets had symbolized. Or, more important, the essence of the person she made those memories with.

Natalie donated the jackets and many of John's other personal effects to a wonderful local nonprofit. And after the last box had been carried out, the room felt empty, but not in a negative way. It felt like a blank canvas. It felt like *possibility*. As we sat on the hardwood floor together, I asked Natalie to dream big about how she wanted to use this freed-up space in this tender new season of life. It didn't take long for her to decide. That next week I helped her transform the spare room into a small but fabulous photography studio for her new business. She was moving forward again, step by step.

That experience with Natalie—which happened early on in my organizing career—stays with me and still affects the way I work with clients today. It brought home to me the invaluable role of empathy in every process, including organizing someone's home. And it illustrated how useful and powerful a tangible tool, like that custom book of photos, can be. That small but significant object became Natalie's bridge, allowing her to move toward a second life, while still remembering and treasuring the first.

SOMETHING TO HOLD ON TO

It's no wonder we humans are drawn to tangible objects when it comes to matters of the heart. Life is an unending series of changes, big and small, sometimes wonderful and sometimes incredibly difficult to bear. We're continually propelled forward and onward through time, ready or not. And we look to the physical—the things we can hold in our hands—to anchor a moment, to pin down a memory and the feelings it gave us, or to be the concrete ties connecting our hearts to someone whose physical presence we've lost.

At their best, sentimental objects serve as small monuments of honor, celebration, or comfort in our lives, bringing back positive memories and feelings of love, joy, or connection every time they're viewed or used. But what's so tricky about objects with emotional ties to the past is that, over time, our relationships to them—and how they affect our present lives— can shift to a taking role rather than a giving role without our awareness. Another way to say it is that you may not be keeping what you *think* you're keeping. That's why it's so important to really take emotional inventory of physical belongings, to reexamine their purpose in our lives.

flip the script
WHAT ARE YOU REALLY TRYING TO KEEP?

When it comes to the belongings of someone we've loved and lost, it can feel nearly impossible to let go, even if the physical and emotional space those items take up is blocking us from growth or the path forward. At these times, it can be helpful to ask yourself, like Natalie did, *"What is it that I am really trying to keep?"* The answer lies beyond the physical object to the intangible. The feelings of love, connection and remembrance, belonging. The very marrow of life.

Julia, one of my clients who had very little storage capacity in her home, had been holding on to her late grandmother's large and bulky sewing machine for more than fifteen years. The problem was that Julia didn't sew, nor did she have any interest in learning to do so in the future. When we explored what she was really trying to hold on to, she began to talk about sitting with her grandmother—the most beloved person in her life as a child—as her grandmother sewed. Just being in her grandmother's gentle presence brought her an immense sense of comfort, connection, acceptance, and love.

Once Julia identified that it was really those good feelings and memories she didn't want to lose, it gave her a little mental space from the object. Suddenly it was easier to see the sewing machine for what it was—a tool she didn't need or use, a tool that someone else could enjoy and make great use of. The exercise also gave Julia permission to admit that she actually felt a little guilty every time she saw the sewing machine sitting there unused. She was surprised to realize that the machine was, in fact, stealing from the happy feelings and memories it was supposed to be preserving.

"So, let's get this straight," she told me. "I've been keeping the thing . . . to never use the thing . . . to be frustrated with the thing for taking up the space where I could've had another thing I would actually use . . . just to have the thing I've been keeping make me feel guilty every day?" We had to laugh. Yet, Julia is far from alone in this crazy scenario. It's so easy to passively participate in a mental loop of hanging on to objects that aren't actually serving us the way we assume they are.

After Julia donated the sewing machine to an organization teaching refugee women how to sew, she took the time to write down what those moments by her grandmother's side had meant to her, what her grandmother meant to her. By intentionally choosing an organization that she knew her grandmother would appreciate, she was able to let the object go with some peace—and with excitement for its next owner. And so in the end, she let go of a bulky item that wasn't serving her or bringing her comfort anymore, and instead found a creative way to give form to her beautiful memories of her grandmother.

THE ACT OF REMEMBERING

What we're asking of mementos from a loved one's life is for them to help us keep that person close. To keep them vibrant in our hearts and lives. We fear that time will fade the felt presence and even the memories of the ones we've loved and lost.

Following my dad's death, my mom held on to his clothes for a long time. I knew they weren't serving her or the rest of the family sitting in a closet or drawers, and I wanted to help her with that transition. I took Dad's clothes and had some of them made into four unique and beautiful quilts—one for Mom, one for me, one for my brother and sister-in-law, and one for my brother's little boy—and we donated the rest.

While I'll always treasure my quilt—that soft, tangible layer of comfort—and believe that physical symbols can be such helpful tools for honoring a life, it's the *act* of remembering that has brought the most healing and comfort to me over the years. Through my clients' stories and my own experiences navigating grief, I've found that often what we're really looking for is intentionality—the assurance that there will be specific ways and times to remember, honor, and celebrate the ones we're missing. Traditions created and observed as an individual or family can be so much more effective at meeting that need than a passive object sitting on a shelf or—worse—in storage. And when decision-making time comes for what to do with a loved one's possessions, the comfort of knowing we have special rituals in place to honor their lives and memories can help to ease the letting go of things we don't love, use, or need.

After my dad passed, every day without him was painful, and certain days, like his birthday and the anniversary of his death, were especially tender. And I expect they always will be. But what helps me, my mom, and my brother is knowing how Dad, the best life celebrator we've ever known, would want us to live and want us to remember him—fully, joyfully embracing every season. As a true Daddy's girl, the loss of my father—my best friend, my mentor, and one of my soulmates—in my early twenties was a tragedy for me. That will always be true. But what is also true, and what helped shape the way I celebrate his life is the perspective that I had twenty-three years of unconditional love, joy, and laughter with him— enough goodness to carry with me for the rest of my days. That's what I think about, especially when his "special days" come back around.

On the anniversary of his death, my mom, my brother, our families, and I always make a point of getting together, even though we don't live close to each other. We make the trip and the effort to be present in each other's lives, to share meals and stories, honoring Dad through it all.

On Dad's birthday, as the big softy of the family, I'm always first to shoot a text to the others that morning, starting the day with "Happy birthday, Dad." My phone buzzes all day with replies: sweet messages and thoughts for and about him. And then that evening, no matter where we all are in the world, we make sure to have his favorite red wine on hand. We end the day with a toast to how well he lived, how deeply we still feel his love, and how our hearts ache with loving him back. Through those simple rituals, combined with the way I try to live on a daily basis, I know I'm honoring Dad's life and how it continues to shape mine. And it makes all the difference.

I've seen friends and clients develop their own traditions around remembering loved ones in countless beautiful and creative ways. As we circle the sun year after year, rituals can hold the space to cherish ones we love in meaningful ways. And while physical things, like my dad's favorite wine, can be wonderful tools, it's the intention and the act of remembering that makes the magic and keeps the sparks of wonderful memories burning bright, giving warmth to our own hearts and others.

INHERITING OR PASSING DOWN KEEPSAKES

Mementos—meant to remind us of a person, time, or place we love—can add beauty, warmth, and meaning to our surroundings. And that is a beautiful thing. I never want to take away from the sense of connection and joy a beloved keepsake can bring. But what I do want to encourage is thoughtful and conscious consideration of each object in your home, even (or especially) keepsakes. Because they're only worth keeping if they add value to your life.

Often, I'll find that my clients are saving mementos that hold no personal meaning or memories for them. But because the objects were treasured by parents, grandparents, or someone from a past generation of their family, the client hangs on to the items out of a sense of loyalty or even obligation. They feel like they *should* value the objects because someone they love did or, at the very least, someone in their lineage passed it down.

Maybe you inherited a giant box of black-and-white photographs, but you can't identify anyone in them.

Or you ended up with your uncle's fly-fishing rod, but you don't fish . . . and you're a vegetarian.

Perhaps your mother gave you all of your grandmother's cookbooks from the 1960s and '70s, but you never met your grandmother and you don't enjoy cooking. And even if you did, you'd probably opt for healthier recipes online, or at least less Velveeta.

Whatever the inherited but unused items list might look like in your life, let me give you this official permission slip: it's not only okay to let go of these items, but in doing so, you'll actually be honoring the lives of your predecessors by living *your* life more fully, free of the excess that takes up needed energy, space, and resources.

Think about it. That's really what every person with goodwill wants for future generations—for them to be able to live a better life than they did. The problem is each generation tends to assume that the next generation will value the same types of possessions they did. It's human nature. But only you can determine what best serves your own life and household.

"MY KIDS WILL WANT THIS SOMEDAY"

I see this all the time: clients hanging on to massive amounts of sentimental objects and all sorts of household goods and furnishings, earnestly maintaining that their kids "will want these things one day."

If there are adult children in the picture, I recommend to the client that we go ahead and reach out to them and confirm that that is indeed the case. Here's the awkward part: the client's children rarely want those fine-china gravy boats, the old set of golf clubs, Mom's wedding dress, a cast from a broken arm when they were eleven (yes, seriously), the Victorian dining-room set, or five bins of photos passed down from Great-aunt Sue. In my experience, 99 percent of the time, the kids just don't want most of it, don't have a use for it, and definitely don't have space for it. Most times, I find that when parents have passed away or are downsizing their estates, adult children want just a few items—their parents' wedding rings, their child-hood photo album, one small piece of furniture, and that walking stick they carved with Dad. And when they do agree to take significant quantities of items off their parents' hands, I find that it's often because they don't want to hurt their parents' feelings. I get it; it's emotionally tricky territory for both parties.

If you find yourself in this situation, either as the parent intending to pass down keepsakes or the child hoping to avoid the burden of excess, you are far from alone. The 2014 United States Census Report projects that more than 20 percent of America's population will be sixty-five or older by 2030.[1] As older adults now, the baby boomer generation is beginning to downsize, moving into smaller, more manageable dwellings or assisted living and retirement communities, which means the volume of unwanted family heirlooms is beginning to grow exponentially. And at the same time, there's been a significant shift in what the next generation values in terms of worldly possessions.

In the 2000s, we started seeing more and more young people move away from clutter and toward minimalist lifestyles. Millennials are embracing smaller living spaces and function over fashion when it comes to furnishings. They are more interested in travel and life experiences than investing in lavish home settings. (A trend I personally love.)

While this dynamic makes for many, many delicate conversations to come on how to handle family keepsakes and heirlooms, I see it as a real opportunity for families to refocus on what really lasts—love, connection, and history shared—when making estate-planning decisions together.

---

1 Jennifer M. Ortman, Victoria A. Velkoff, and Howard Hogan, "Table 2: Projections and Distribution of the Total Population by Age for the United States: 2012 to 2050," in *An Aging Nation: The Older Population in the United States* (Washington, DC: US Census Bureau Reports, May 2014), *https://www.census.gov/content/dam/Census/library/publications/2014/demo/p25-1140.pdf.*

If you're an older parent seeking to downsize, it's natural to want to share what you have with someone you love—to give what you found valuable to the people you most value: your children. But sharing is a two-way street, and if you are putting your own worth into the belongings you wish to pass down, it will be easy to feel rejected if your children prefer not to become their new owners.

For adult children trying to navigate this scenario: if you have the room in your current living situation *and* any of the intended items bring you joy, cherish them as long as they do just that. But if you don't, be gentle and firm with your "No, thank you." Reassure your parents that the intangible legacy of love is the greatest treasure they can pass down, and then be free.

A FEW OF YOUR FAVORITE THINGS

Childhood treasures are among the most nostalgic of all the items we hang on to, certainly for the parent and often for the grown-up child his or herself. Those tender years are so fleeting, after all.

As a bachelor in his late thirties, my client, Drew, deeply wanted to have a family of his own. He could hardly wait to marry a sweet lady and make some beautiful babies. In particular, he was dreaming about having a son one day, a little buddy with whom to throw a baseball and share all of his favorite things.

When Drew reached out to Life in Jeneral, he wanted help turning his bachelor pad into a more welcoming space for hosting guests. Everything about organizing Drew's home went quickly and smoothly until I came to the guest-room closet overflowing with sentimental objects from his childhood. His parents had recently retired and subsequently downsized, which meant that Drew had been the recipient of bins and bins of boyhood items he hadn't seen in more than twenty years. Clothes, toys, music, books, and odds and ends galore.

With each bin we opened, you could see the nostalgia and happy boyhood memories wash over Drew, a self-professed sentimental guy. Yes, it all took up a lot of space, he admitted, but these G.I. Joe figures were surely collectibles by now, right? The items that took up the most real estate were the dozens and dozens of cassettes, VHS tapes, and DVDs. No, he told me, he couldn't let these go. They were still his favorites, and he was so excited by the thought of sharing them with his future son in the same way (read: outdated format) he had enjoyed them as a boy. The problem was all of this boyhood paraphernalia was taking up the very space he wanted to make more hospitable for others in his current life—for those visits he wanted to encourage from family members and old friends.

I asked Drew to think about what he was *really* wanting to keep by holding on to all these sentimental objects? What were the intangible things he wanted to preserve for, and share with, his future son?

Drew concluded that it was about *sharing the experience* of the things that had brought him so much enjoyment growing up. He realized it wasn't actually the physical plastic cassettes and VHS tapes that were important to him; it was the songs and the stories, all of which could be acquired digitally and save him a ton of shelf space. I recommended that Drew make a list of all of the music and movies from this collection on his phone before letting go of the physical copies. He liked that idea. He could relax knowing that his list of favorites was only a digital file away on that happy day when it felt it was time to share them. (Thank you, Spotify, iTunes, and the rest.)

In the end, Drew was able to narrow down his favorite childhood items to one bin at the top of the guest closet. Not only did the process leave plenty of space for linens and blankets for guests to use, it also helped him hone in on what was most special to him—his old baseball jerseys, a beloved old bear, and a few iconic toys—and *why*. By being selective about what he saved, the items he chose to keep felt even more meaningful.

The memory box (or bin) is a practice that has helped many of my clients. I love the idea of a single place where your most cherished memorabilia is stored. Because we begin to devalue objects that we have in excess, less really is more. It brings more awareness of what you have and a sweeter sentiment toward it. Let's narrow down all the keepsakes to those that really make your heart shine, instead of keeping so many that you can't remember what they are, much less get them out to share and enjoy.

A brief note on saving physical items from special events or milestones: a good rule of thumb is to choose the items that take up the least amount of circumference. Let's say you were the first-generation college graduate in your family and it feels really important to you to save a tangible symbol from commencement. Consider saving just the tassel, not the whole mortarboard and robe. And remember that photos and writing can be the best memory triggers of all.

KEEPING PERSPECTIVE WITH KEEPSAKES

If sentimental objects, keepsakes, or passed-down heirlooms have been tricky decision-making territory for you in the past, don't forget to ask yourself what intangible worth (i.e., good feelings that contribute to your well-being) they bring to your life. Are they actively bringing you joy? Do they remind you of the extraordinary moment or the irreplaceable person they're meant to represent?

Here are some other helpful questions and prompts to use when deciding whether or not to keep objects with emotional ties:

- Are there any other feelings wrapped up in this object besides joy and affection? Guilt for not using or displaying it or letting it remain in a state of disrepair? If feelings of shame, regret, or disappoint emerge, the item could be holding you in the past. Look a little closer.

- Will it be stored or will you use or display it? If the former, strongly consider giving it away to someone who would enjoy it, or donating it to charity.

- If the item feels essential to save, ask yourself *why*. Your answer should line up with the person you want to be and the home atmosphere you seek to create.

- Are there other objects in your possession that serve the same emotional purpose (e.g., make you think of the same person, place, or experience) but take up less physical space? Consider focusing on those and letting the bigger objects go.

- Plan for the space you have today. If sentimental items are taking up needed space, capture the feelings they offer through photographs or writing, and narrow items down to your true favorites (e.g., to one memory box instead of ten).

i might need it
some day

BECOME FULLY ALIVE TO THE PRESENT AS YOU STOP
TRYING TO CONTROL THE FUTURE.

One of the tricky if not humorous parts of my profession is that, as an organizer, you're always a little bit "on trial" to see if the professional advice you give out will really hold up and pan out in your own home and life beyond the job.

While writing this book, my best friend's twelve-year-old daughter, Brynn, wanted to have a sleepover at my house. The request was not unusual—our families are super close, and I always feel flattered to be that "extra mom" figure. But this time Brynn wanted to also invite a friend from school. If anyone's counting, that's two *preteen* girls over for a slumber party. No pressure. (Okay, there was definitely pressure. I really wanted it to be a special time for Brynn and her friend. You know, the kind where they tell their friends how *not* lame Aunt Jen is.)

Both the girls love to cook, so we decided to go all out and make home-made pasta for dinner. There we were in the kitchen with aprons on and the dough ready to roll . . . and it was at that moment that I suddenly remembered I had gotten rid of my KitchenAid pasta roller attachment just a few months prior when moving into my new home. It took up cabinet space, and I had never used or needed it . . . until this exact moment. Gulp.

I will admit that there was a panicky moment of feeling like one of my organizing philosophies had finally backfired and that I would probably never live this down within our family circle: "Of course Jen would purge the pasta roller right before we decide to do a pasta night." But after a couple of eye rolls in my direction and a little laughter at my expense, out came the rolling pin. It took me and the girls (all newbies at pasta making) at least an hour longer than it should have to roll out the dough by hand. And you know what? It was so much fun. Not only was dinner delicious but the extra time talking and laughing in the kitchen together ended up being the highlight of the night. Crisis averted.

THE TROUBLE WITH SAVING THINGS FOR "SOMEDAY"

Most people use up a significant amount of home and storage space just trying to avoid awkward moments like my pasta-roller scenario. In fact, of all the reasons my clients give for holding on to things, "I might need it someday" is the rationale I hear most. In a 2016 survey published by the storage-service locator SpareFoot, "in case I need them in the future" was the number-one reason participants from seven major US cities cited as why they kept items they didn't use or need.[2]

No one, myself included, wants to find themselves in a situation where they feel unprepared or ill-equipped. The instinct to use possessions as protection against vulnerability surely goes all the way back to our very beginning as humans, when basic resources were much more difficult to come by. *Hang on to whatever you've got, no matter what!* But while we're no longer living in caves or having to chase down dinner with a spear, our natural instincts for self-preservation—if not checked—go into overdrive, and we can easily find ourselves rationalizing the storage of all kinds of random objects for a false sense of security. Things like:

- unused rice cookers, juicers, bread makers, yogurt makers, and generally all the makers
- expired medications, makeup, lotions, spices, and fire extinguishers (tip: *Most things actually have a finite shelf life*)
- enough backstock products and paper goods to supply a small fortress (see tip above)
- Halloween costumes for kids and adults that they never plan to wear again
- drawers of freebie conference or event swag (all those branded pens, stickers, flash drives, and koozies have got to come in handy one day, right?)
- excessive amounts of office supplies
- wedding dresses (saved for daughters, whether they want them or not)

2 Wakefield Research, *SpareFoot Survey: QuickRead Report* (Austin, Texas: SpareFoot, 2016), https://www.sparefoot.com/self-storage/blog/wp-content/uploads/sites/2/2016/05/Wakefield-Research-QuickRead-Report-for-SpareFoot.pdf.

- dozens of flower vases (in cabinets, not holding flowers)
- boxes of defunct electronics (because one day we'll find another use for that indestructible Nokia "brick" phone)
- craft items purchased for projects we no longer feel inspired to complete
- large amounts of extra linens (enough for an army of guests)
- outdated sports equipment
- multiple suitcases in duplicate sizes
- clothing that's too small

This list is a small sampling of the most common items my clients save "just in case," but the variety and scale of clutter that's kept for no *logical* reason is truly limitless. One of my clients couldn't throw away paper clips because they "could be useful one day." I estimated his collection at around ten thousand clips. Not kidding.

Another client's chest of drawers was stuffed with thirty pairs of the same black yoga pants just in case that company ever stopped making her favorite kind.

Then there was the gentleman who would compulsively buy candles and other gift-type items he found on sale to stock his gift closet. "That way, I'm not empty-handed when it's appropriate to bring a hostess a gift or I forget someone's birthday is coming up soon," he explained. The problem was the gift closet was overflowing. It turned out he had never once accessed this stash for a quickly needed present. He simply bought something else when the time came.

While the types of clutter may vary greatly, most of us are guilty of stock-piling *something* in an effort to prevent life from cornering us in a position of lack.

flip the script
WHAT ARE YOU SO AFRAID OF?

At one time or another, we've all fallen victim to the fear that we won't have what we need when we need it. And we're especially afraid of regret. We've all gotten rid of things, only to wish we hadn't later. That little bit of doubt is all your brain needs to shift into self-preservation-plus mode, to tell you to hold on to clutter even if it's taking over your house or blocking you from the life you want to be living today.

If fear of regret or future lack is keeping you from letting go of things, the best thing you can do is to face it head on. Ask yourself: *"What am I so afraid of? What is the worst thing that could happen if I let this item go?"* Then let yourself imagine the worst-case scenario and determine what your options would be at that point. Most of the time, even that first, simple step can feel like a relief because you're no longer spending the energy trying to avoid those thoughts. Simply allowing your mind to go there and exploring your fears can dispel anxiety that's been pent up with no outlet.

So I purge my KitchenAid pasta-roller attachment and then forget about it until I'm in the middle of hosting a pasta-making night with two preteens. Then what? We make up a plan B on the fly, look up "rolling out pasta dough" on YouTube, and grab the rolling pin. If that doesn't work, we'll order pizza. And that would be okay too. The point is we would survive. When you're focused on what (and who!) matters most to you, the "worst-case scenario" can still be a pretty great option.

As an organizer, I never promise clients they won't need or someday want something they've purged. The truth is, whether it's six months or six years down the road, you probably *will* need something you got rid of while organizing. We can only make educated guesses on how life will unfold, after all. All the more reason to focus on what you *do* know you need in your life now. You can't control the future, but you can free up mental and physical space to more fully live into the present.

Most of the time, you'll find that the panic over someday not having something when you need it is *way* worse than the reality of that situation. If I had to choose all over again how the girls' night with Brynn would go, I would do it the same way. I would happily give up a box of seldom-used kitchen tools, gathering dust in the cabinet, to gain that extra hour of bonding with the girls. Because, in the end, using our creativity made the process way more fun than it might have been to simply pull the pasta-roller attachment out of the box.

RESOURCEFULNESS COMES FROM WITHIN

One of the mindsets than can stick with you even more than the fear of regret is the idea that holding on to items in case you need them one day is resourceful. On a surface level, it's not difficult to see why this is an easy association to make. Isn't holding on to something so you don't have to spend money repurchasing it later a form of frugality?

Well, not exactly. This certainly isn't true if the item is costing you space that you could better use to meet your current goals. It's not true if there is an intangible tax (mental energy, maintenance, time spent tidying, etc.) included in holding on to the object, which there always is in some form. And it's definitely not true if you are paying to store it.

For those who grew up in households where the admonition "Don't be wasteful" was said pretty much daily, it can be particularly difficult to release possessions that could possibly be useful someday. But consider this perspective: allowing underused belongings to sit and depreciate in value (and often in function) when someone else could be using or enjoying them is wasteful too. A much healthier approach is to appreciate the excitement that that item brought into your life when you first received or purchased it, and then donate it or pass it on.

Resourcefulness is *not* having whatever you could possibly need before you possibly need it. That's a fantasy. True resourcefulness comes from within. It's the ability to swiftly and skillfully deal with new challenges as they arise. In other words, a resourceful person is a problem solver.

Don't get me wrong: if homemade pasta suddenly became a regular menu item in my household, I wouldn't hesitate to purchase a new KitchenAid attachment. But for most situations in life, there is more than one solution. If an item you purge becomes useful later, it will likely be available again, and in a variety of ways. If you need an item for temporary use, borrow or rent the object instead of purchasing it this time. Look for a substitute or another way of achieving the same end results.

The truth is that nobody can prepare for or avoid all possible problems. And I'm not sure that's what life's really about anyway. As humans, our incredible brains were made to turn things over. When our minds are creatively engaged in finding solutions, that's when we come alive. That's when we thrive.

What are the most memorable parts of a cross-country road trip, a camping excursion, or navigating the subway system in an unfamiliar city? The parts that didn't go as planned. The unexpected snags. These are the moments we laugh about later—the parts of the story we love to retell through the years. Somehow we fumbled around until we figured it out. And then we kept going. That's what makes an adventure, after all.

Every time we rise to the occasion, however imperfectly, we're building confidence that we can do it again. And the more we trust our own resourcefulness, the more we can travel through this life with lightness and joy. Sometimes that means your arms ache from rolling out pounds of pasta dough, but hey—totally worth it.

PARTY OVER PERFECT

What about items you fully intend to use for a specific purpose or event one day but—for whatever reason—you just haven't done it yet? The truth is, if this thing you really mean to do doesn't have a deadline or isn't on the calendar, you may have already waited too long. From what I've seen in my clients' lives, I'm convinced that much of the time *keeping the thing keeps you from doing the thing.* I swear, it's some kind of ironic universal rule.

If you met my client Liza, you'd be having a great time after about three minutes of her company. Lively, vibrant, welcoming, and funny, Liza is your classic life-of-the-party lady. And that's why it didn't surprise me when I saw several bins and shelves of party supplies in her garage for a big Hawaiian-themed bash she was planning to throw with the help of her husband, Jordan. But the more rooms my team and I worked through for the couple, the more party paraphernalia we found tucked away. Tiki torches and authentic tiki masks. Gorgeous conch shells for centerpieces. Large, colorful ceramic planters for the hibiscus plants she'd bring in before the party. You name it.

I asked Liza when she was going to throw this epic celebration for her friends. "I'm not sure yet," she replied a little sheepishly. "It just never seems to be the right time." That's when Jordan gave her the side-eye.

"Tell Jen how long you've been planning this party," he prompted. Turns out, Liza had been collecting stuff for this festive affair during her travels or shopping trips for close to ten years. She had clung to the idea for so long it had become almost unattainable in her own mind. The very stuff she had bought to make her dream a reality had become the barrier. Without her realizing it, her real inspiration and motivation to actually host the event had waned. Liza couldn't admit that, though. It felt like too much of a defeat to let go of all the cool things it had taken almost a decade to collect.

I knew that it was now or never for Liza to use her carefully curated collection, so—no joke—I offered to help her throw the party myself, free of charge. We could organize it together. Let's do this thing. "Oh, that's okay," she demurred. It wasn't good timing, after all.

When an idea becomes too precious, we can limit our own creative energy and will to act. Seriously, nothing kills creativity and momentum like planning for perfection. But when we can own that the timing for a certain dream has passed, sit with disappointment, and then muster the courage to let go of the physical items that symbolize that dream, we open ourselves up to new inspiration.

I recognized the moment that Liza turned down voluntary help from a professional organizer to finally throw the "party of her dreams" that she had been gearing up for all these years as a "pull back the curtain" moment—a chance to pause—and invited Liza to see where her mindset was really at, what she really wanted to do or not do, and why. In the end, Liza was able to admit, "If this has become so big in my mind that I'm not even willing to put in on the calendar with a professional team helping me pull it off, maybe this isn't going to happen."

What did she do instead? Liza was able to let go of some of the Hawaiian party decor, and she used what she kept to throw a small (but fabulous and fun!) island-themed birthday for her young daughter the next month. There were just a few guests—a handful of children from her daughters' class, and their parents—and a very well-known Disney island princess may or may not have made an appearance. Liza's little girl was over the moon, and it doesn't get better than that kind of delight.

When I followed up with Liza a couple months later, she shared how much fun she had throwing a simple party. This was her jam: entertaining and making people feel special, whatever the scale. She had no regrets about letting her "collection" go, or be used in a different way than she had planned—it had allowed her to resolve something that had her stuck, that had her more focused on props than on actually bringing people together. But she still wanted to do something big: an event to remember, but without a decade of lead-up. The last I heard, Liza had roped in a group of friends to help plan and pull off a big charity bash for one of their favorite causes. I don't know what the theme is, but I have every confidence that *this* party is going to happen.

If you've waited a long time for the perfect moment, family situation, or set of circumstances to use something you've been saving, it's probably not going to happen. Maybe you've built a certain dream up in your mind such that there's no way carrying out the real thing could ever live up to the fantasy version. This mentality winds up blocking you from other greatness. You start to think, "Well, I didn't finish *this*, so how can I ever start *that*?"

My advice is to check in with yourself. Your desire, your energy, or the general opportunity to pull this thing off may have passed without your realizing it. It's okay to let the stuff go and let someone else throw one kick-ass Hawaiian party with your fabulously curated decor.

But if you decide you still *really* want to do whatever it is, forgo the fanfare and do it now. Like today or tomorrow, or next weekend at the latest. Put it on the calendar, enlist the help of some friends, and throw that party. Set up that home gym. Host that workshop. Do whatever it is promptly, imperfectly, and gladly.

Otherwise, let go of both the idea and the supplies. Then open your hands and get ready to catch the new inspiration that's coming your way, because now you've made room for it. This time, you'll be ready to act on it.

HOLDING ON TO HOPE

Sometimes we have a dream that, try as we might, isn't actually in our power to fulfill. This is particularly true for hopeful parents who are navigating the bewildering pain of infertility, loss, and endless waiting. In these situations, preserving items that represent this sacred hope can be a good and helpful thing to do. But how you do it can make all the difference for your present life and heart.

One of the most tender and vulnerable moments I've shared with a client was spent sitting on the floor of what was meant to be a nursery. After years of wading through the wilderness of infertility treatments, Amy and her loving spouse, Ryan, were elated to become pregnant. But when Amy called me for help with her home, they had lost the pregnancy five months prior.

As we sat there talking, our backs to the wall where a crib was meant to be, my heart broke to witness even a small portion of this woman's unknowable pain. And yet somehow there was hope mingled in with the grief. They wanted to try again for a baby in the future, Amy shared through tears, but not yet.

She had been well into the second trimester before the miscarriage, and their tiny girl already had a name, her own room in their home, and clothes and gifts in the closet. That was the space where the sadness was most palpable.

"I don't like to come in here," Amy confided. "The ache is just too much when I see all of her things, but I can't let them go. It would feel like I was letting *her* go." And what about all the baby equipment and things that had been gifted to them, things they hoped to use for a baby in the future?

She wanted and needed to remember and to heal, both at the same time.

I suggested to Amy that we have a beautiful wooden keepsake box created just for her daughter. The most cherished possessions went there—the little fuzzy lamb, the silver cross bracelet for christening day, and the soft blanket Amy's grandmother had had embroidered with their daughter's name. Then we got a single large bin, and Amy and Ryan selected a few of the supplies and equipment that felt most important to them for a baby in the future, and we took both the memory box and the bin out of the nursery and put them on the top shelf in the corner of their bedroom closet. We were able to pack up the rest of the items in the room, and Amy gifted them to a dear friend who was expecting. It gave her comfort to know that the items would be used by someone she dearly cared about.

When we talked a few days later, Amy shared with me how consolidating and moving the items out of the former nursery closet had somehow brought an immediate sense of relief. It was deeply comforting to know the things were tucked safely and obscurely away for when she wanted or needed them. But now she could walk down the hall without feeling the same weight come over her every time she passed that room or needed to get something out of the closet.

Soon afterward, Amy and Ryan repainted the little room that will hopefully be a nursery again one day. For now, they've remade it into a guest room, meant especially to host Amy's mom—someone she wants extra time with, now more than ever.

For anyone experiencing the deep vulnerability of loss *while* simultaneously holding on to hope for the future in that same area, one of the bravest things you can do is take good care of yourself in the meantime. Let your decision on what you keep in your home (and where and how) be guided by what will actually most nurture your heart in this particular season.

One of the big things to remember when it comes to this barrier of saving things for "one day" is that nobody can predict the future. It's totally normal to want to hold on to items just in case you eventually need them, but while you're waiting for that day to come, you're living in a home that mostly makes you think of the future. If you set up your home in a way that helps you stay grounded in the present, you'll be able to look forward with more excitement and far less pressure.

i'd feel guilty
if i let this go

TRADE GUILT FOR GRATEFULNESS,
NO STRINGS ATTACHED.

Growing up, Brady had one of the toughest inner-city childhoods you can imagine. And like many kids who endure trauma, his way of coping was to keep everything light, laugh at himself as much as possible, and make others laugh too. He was brilliant at it. Brady was also incredibly resourceful and resilient, and his talent for comedy took him all the way to celebrity status. When his fame and income level began to increase at a rapid rate, instead of upgrading his square footage, Brady chose to remain in a modest-size home in the neighborhood he grew up in. It was his way of remaining connected to his roots and family and not losing touch with where he came from. He simply felt most at home there. Or at least he had, until things began up piling up.

The more successful Brady became in the industry, the more physical stuff seemed to come through his door (and post office box), and the more unhappy he began to feel in his own house. When his mother fell ill, Brady took her in to live with him without a second thought. He was happy to have the means to care for her, but this meant that his small space became even more condensed and the rising level of clutter felt even more unbearable. After sharing the situation with his manager, they reached out to me for help.

"What could be keeping this resilient young man, who has already over-come so much, from accomplishing his goal for an organized and peaceful home?" I wondered while driving to his house. Only ten minutes and two rooms into the site visit, I knew a big part of the answer: unwanted gifts and guilt.

There were heaps of clothing, watches, jewelry, luggage, grooming prod-ucts, and more, and almost all of it was untouched. Brady confided that he didn't need or want to store these things, but he felt weird about letting any of it go. They were *gifts*, after all. And whether they were congratulatory tokens from fellow celebrities, presents from fans, or fancy products from business owners, Brady felt obligated to hang on to the items, even if he didn't plan to—or think he could—use them. "I'd just feel like a jerk getting rid of them after they spent the time and money on me," he said. "Plus, I'll never forget what it felt like to have nothing, and I don't want to take these things for granted."

Ironically, the very definition of a gift—something given voluntarily without payment in return—flies in the face of feeling like we owe some-thing back, like we owe the physical and mental space needed to keep the item in our home. A sense of indebtedness can bind us to what we were given, making the objects more difficult to part with.

What does it take to shake free? Choosing gratitude instead of guilt for a kindness offered, and tapping into our own self-worth—claiming agency in our own lives.

Brady and I had a lot to unpack together, and not just the dozens of boxes of gifts. But thankfully, he was ready to do some soul work around what these new belongings were bringing up for him, especially if it meant he could love his small house again—and feel at home in his own skin again, too.

WHO'S WRITING THE STORY?

Holding on to things out of guilt can be a signal that we have yet to take ownership of our own stories. Brady's anchor was his history of overcoming. He began to share how *he* had been the one to positively build up his life through his own choices, hard work, and honing of his craft. *He* was the one taking care of his mother's medical bills. *He* had chosen to stay in a small home in a neighborhood that may have seemed rough to an outsider but meant something to him. It's not that Brady hadn't found support and good friendships along the way, but this was *his* story to write, and—as he talked—it was like he was remembering all over again that he was writing it well.

What's interesting is, not long before hiring me to organize his home, Brady had gotten a lot of press for sharing openly about his impoverished upbringing and his journey to a self-made (and highly successful) career. But for some reason, he hadn't been able to transfer that sense of identity in his professional life over to how he interacted with his home. He felt indebted to the influential people who had sent him these nice things. But the more Brady tuned into his role in his own story, the more he began to make the connection that not only was he worthy of the gifts, he was worthy of the right to keep or let them go as he saw fit. (And so, by the way, are you.) I knew that Brady had made a breakthrough with his relationship to these possessions when he said, "Having nothing didn't define me in the past, and now the ability to have 'everything' doesn't define me either."

The role you play in your own story dictates how you'll receive gifts and view the possessions in your life in general. Do you own them or the other way around?

RECEIVING AND RELEASING UNWANTED GIFTS

Most of us aren't navigating an onslaught of swag due to celebrity status, but gifts can make up a significant amount of traffic and inventory in any home. Holiday and birthday presents. Seasonal cheer. Thank-you gifts. Congratulations and acknowledgements. I-just-thought-of-you-when-I-saw-it gifts. They add up to a lot of new influx into a home, on a monthly, weekly, or even more frequent basis.

Whatever the occasion, it feels good to be thought of. And isn't that what the giving is all about anyway? We know that not everything we're gifted will support our lifestyles, tastes, or goals for our homes. Yet, when it's time to release or repurpose a gift, we often still choke on the guilt around getting rid of the physical object rather than simply appreciating the intention behind it. For my clients, the dilemma usually takes at least one of two forms: they don't want to hurt the giver's feelings, or they don't want to be or seem ungrateful.

When it comes to discarding unwanted gifts, there's a common fear (yup, there's fear lurking, in some form, behind every barrier) that the giver will check up on us and will be hurt when they find that we are not using or displaying their gift. The truth is, most of the time that just doesn't happen. It's all in our heads.

Think about it: When you bring someone a bottle of wine to thank them for hosting you, do you ask them later, "So, did you drink that bottle of wine I brought you? How'd you like it?" No, that would be awkward. Or, after you give a decorative item to a friend, do you comb through their home the next time you pay a visit to see if it's on display? I hope not.

If someone does inquire about a gift they gave you after the fact, it's typically a close relationship. Your mom, mother-in-law, or bestie. Frankly, if she or he feels comfortable enough to ask after the gift, she or he is probably someone you could be honest with about your goals for your lifestyle and home when it comes to simplifying your possessions, right? (More on this in just a bit!)

Still need some reassurance? Putting yourself in the shoes of the giver can help too. The truth is, they wouldn't want their gift to collect dust on your shelf or in your closet. And they wouldn't want you to keep it only out of guilt either.

flip the script
WHAT IS THE ACTUAL PURPOSE OF GIVING AND RECEIVING?

Gifts, in their purest form, after all, are simply meant to demonstrate our care for one another. And if something is given for any other reason than to simply bring pleasure, delight, joy, or comfort to the recipient, then it's not a gift; it's something trying to get something from you—whether that's attention, affection, or gratitude. (And, in that case, there's probably a bigger issue at stake than not wanting to hurt the feelings of someone important to you.)

When you're struggling to release a gift because of guilt, go back to the real purpose of giving and receiving and ask yourself: *"Did I receive this gift with gratefulness because someone thought of me?"* If the answer is yes, hooray! The gift has served its purpose, and you can let it move on. If you never paused to appreciate the thought behind the item, it's not too late—you can give thanks for the thoughtfulness of the gift *while* placing the item in the donate pile. I'm serious!

Gratefulness is an attitude of the heart; it has nothing to do with keeping a physical object. And how cool would it be if we let even the act of simplifying our possessions remind us of the times people in our lives showed they care?

The practice of snipping any "strings" attached to objects we receive from others—whether they are real or projected out of our own fears or insecurities—builds our joy muscles because joyful living isn't dependent on others' expectations. It grows from personal satisfaction with gratefulness at the roots. And the bonus benefit to changing the way we receive things (sans the condition of "keeping" them) is that, inevitably, there will be less strings attached in our own giving as well.

WHEN A PURCHASE WAS A MISTAKE

Guilt can also be a barrier when it comes to discarding items that we purchased but never or rarely used. We hate to admit that our choice was a waste of money, and so we hold on to the object to justify the purchase. We've all been there. It can be a real blow to realize how much money we've spent giving in to marketing, making an impulse buy, or simply making a bad guess about what our future selves would want or need. Instead of punishing yourself by feeling guilty every time you see an item you *thought* you'd need, let the fumble teach you something about the kinds of things you do and don't actually use or wear.

So show yourself the same thoughtfulness you would when picking an item for someone else. You know that great feeling of watching and waiting for just the right gift for someone you love—something that is right up their alley? It's such a lift! You deserve that treatment from yourself too. And by more thoughtfully considering what it is you're bringing into the home, you're almost guaranteed to buy less (so your bank account won't mind it either).

WHAT NOW?

One of the key things that helped Brady move past the guilt of not keeping the multitude of gifts that were sent to him was finding a new purpose for them, one that meant a lot to him. Having experienced homelessness at more than one point in his life before adulthood, Brady decided that he would take any excess toiletries, clothing, or other youth-appropriate items he received and create care packages for the kids served by a local homeless shelter. As someone who grew up with secondhand everything, it gave him immense satisfaction that the repurposed gifts were high-quality and, most important, new. Everything he sends over to the shelter—yes, he's still doing it today and loving it—is sealed, packaged, or has the tags still on.

You can take a similarly intentional approach to organizing your home. Once you've completed the first step—letting go of the guilt—you need to figure out what will keep the gifts from accumulating in your home again.

Next step? Be proactive. Have a plan for what you're going to do when the inevitable gifts that don't fit your needs or lifestyle arrive. Determine what kinds of items can be repurposed or regifted—if you're not a candle person, for example, maybe you decide to regift any nice candles you receive as thank-you or hostess gifts. Identify your favorite local charities and what kind of items they can use. Keep in mind that there is gratitude to be found, and you can let go of guilt by sharing items that will make someone else happy—yes, someone *will* be grateful to have that bright-pink sweater Aunt Suzy knitted, it doesn't have to be you!

owning your story, SHARING YOUR NEW GOALS

Make a list of the people close to you, the ones you receive gifts from most often. And before your next birthday or the next gift-centric holiday (whichever comes first!), share your journey toward a more organized home and simpler life with them. Give them ideas for the kinds of gifts that would be meaningful and useful to your home life right now. Maybe the ideal gift is not an object at all, but an experience—a massage, a concert, a workshop on creating charcuterie boards, guitar lessons, or simply *time* together. Don't hesitate to get specific and make a wish list that they can pull from whenever. Honestly, they'll probably be relieved to know exactly what to get you. It'll save them time and energy, and it will make them happy to know that their gift to you is just right.

A few years ago, I had to gather my own courage to communicate my desires and boundaries around receiving gifts to someone I love most in the world: my mom. My mother is truly one of the most thoughtful people in the world, and as such, she is also the care-package queen. In our family and our friend circle, she is well known for constantly sending little things to the people she loves—for celebratory occasions, for holidays (even the minor ones), and "just because." Valentine's candy. Clover-antennae head-bands for Saint Patrick's Day. Emoji-covered notebooks. Guys, I'm telling you, my mom is single-handedly keeping the United States Postal Service in business, all just to put a smile on people's faces.

But here is the rub: for years, I was one of her most frequent recipients of these packages. Depending on the trinkets, I could sometimes regift or donate them, but I hated the thought of my mom spending her money and energy on sending things that I couldn't or wouldn't use. And, frankly, I didn't want to pass clutter on to others. I decided to tell her the truth about the situation as gently as could. I let Mom know that her thoughtfulness was one of my favorite traits about her and that I loved the notes and cards that accompanied those care packages, but that I didn't need and couldn't use the trinkets she was sending. "I know you love to show me you care by getting me things," I remember saying. "How about getting dinner next time I'm in town instead? I would love that."

To Mom's credit, she received everything I had to say so graciously. She rarely sends care packages these days, and when she does they now come simply in the form of cards or notes or maybe gift cards with a little money to use at places I like, and it always makes my whole day—not just receiving the gift, but what she chose to put inside shows she heard me and she gets me. She does tease me about that conversation, though. But I don't mind. It's kind of our running joke now.

Because, let's be real, when gift-giving is your love language, it isn't al-ways the most fun to have a professional organizer for a daughter. I can own that. My mom has given me, after all, one fantastic example of secure love, of the willingness to adjust the tangible way you care for someone in order to show that you value their goals and boundaries because you value *them.* In communicating my boundaries gently and firmly, and staying true to my own path and relationship to physical possessions, I feel more aware of wanting to give space for others to do that. And, I hope, like Mom, I have the security, grace, and willingness to adjust how I show I care for others when needed, too.

Beyond the goal of minimizing waste or deterring incoming clutter, understanding the needs you have for your space and communicating honestly about those goals is a way of owning your story, just as Brady did—and it'll allow you to build a more organized and more joyful home. It's a way of more deeply staking your claim on the kind of existence you're seeking to create. Be gracious but unapologetic in the telling of it. Because, in the end, you're the only one who can (and gets to) make and remake your own life, and you don't need to feel any guilt about that.

i'd feel lost
without my stuff

LEAVE SPACE TO FIND YOURSELF.

Okay, I'm just going to put it out there from the get-go: the barrier we're exploring in this chapter can be a real beast to break through. And that's because it takes a great deal of self-awareness to recognize when your relationship with your belongings has become confused with your sense of self-worth, or even with your sense of self.

Most of my clients are able to identify when they are holding on to something because they're sentimentally attached to it or they believe they "might need it someday." But it's much more difficult for them to pinpoint when they're relying on possessions to tell themselves (or others) who they are, shield themselves from emotional discomfort, or offer lasting security. That's a lot to ask of any physical object, and yet I see it happen every day.

But there's good news: while the journey toward discovering that *you are enough without your stuff* might require some deeper soul work, it doesn't have to be a downer or a slog. In fact, the first steps can be surprisingly simple and full of hope.

EMILY'S STORY

For Emily, everything seemed to change overnight. One day she was part of the quintessential family of four, buzzing along to keep up with her eight-year-old son's and twelve-year-old daughter's many activities. And the next day, her husband was packing a couple of bags with a portion of his clothes and the few belongings he wanted to take with him, and he was gone.

In the wake of a divorce she never wanted, only one thing kept Emily's nose above water, and that was her fierce desire to protect the kids. If she had had the financial means, Emily would have packed up the kids, bought another home close to her mother, and started over. But she didn't have that flexibility. All she knew, she said when she called me, was that she needed to find a way to help the kids know that they would be okay. She asked for my help to make that house a home again, for the three of them.

It takes some kind of primal courage to reach out right in the middle of your most vulnerable state, in the middle of heartbreak, for the help to rebuild your life. That's the grit of a mama bear. As my team and I began working in her home, it seemed easy for Emily to make decisions about purging and organizing the family-centric rooms and the kids' spaces in the house. But when we got to the master suite, it was a different story.

The *his* and *hers* sides of the closet, sides of the bed, and sides of the bathroom vanity that she had never given a second thought to before now made her want to run. Her husband's exit was so recent that his abandoned clothes were still on the hangers, and the toiletries he'd left behind were still on the counter and in the vanity drawers. As we cleared his items away, it was obvious that the quantity of Emily's belongings wouldn't fill the vacancies. At first, that was really uncomfortable for her. The empty drawers and shelves felt like depressing reminders of who was missing, and what was broken. In some ways, the presence of his belongings—even while turning her inside-out—had given Emily some vague sense of security, like maybe this was all a bad dream. If his stuff was still there, he couldn't really be gone, could he? The blank spaces where the objects had once been, on the other hand, felt scary. Too vulnerable.

As we talked through it, I reassured Emily that we would remake the master suite to be all her own, and beautiful for use. We would make her closet a little showroom that she could shop every morning, and we'd spread her personal effects out—give them space to breathe. But I also gently challenged Emily to let some of those vacant drawers and shelves stay that way for now, to resist the urge to buy things just to fill them, just to avoid the emptiness. I encouraged her to view the empty places as her holding space—both literally and figuratively—for something good ahead.

HOLD SPACE FOR YOURSELF

Emily's initial unease with the empty drawers and shelves was far from unique among my clients, no matter their home or life situations. It often takes conscious restraint on their parts to not automatically repopulate any free space that becomes available. When excess and overflow is what feels normal, when we seem to "never have enough" storage capacity for all the clutter, having more space than stuff almost feels wrong—like we're lacking something, but we don't know what. And so it's easier to just add one thing here . . . and then another thing *there* . . . and then, without realizing it, you've eliminated all of your free space.

As you enter the work of simplifying your home and letting excess go, let me be the one to tell you that it's okay to have an empty drawer, empty shelf, or empty whatever! Not only is it okay, but that newly vacant spot offers an opportunity. Give yourself time to see what lasting needs or desires surface instead of rushing to fill every nook with things just to know that they're filled. Sure, emptiness of any kind can feel awkward or uncomfortable. But remember that the need to fill a space can be a way of avoiding discomfort, of having to really think through what you need and how you want a space to feel. If you choose to sit with that discomfort awhile, you'll find that thinking more about your own goals allows you to unlock new perspectives. Ask yourself: *"Am I willing to be temporarily uncomfortable for the chance to gain insight that could ultimately bring more lasting satisfaction into my life?"* If you can make asking this question a practice, the resulting benefits will go way beyond what you choose to fill your physical spaces with.

For Emily, having just gone through such a traumatic event, it made all the sense in the world that she would want to normalize the situation. Adding things and filling space can make us feel like everything is fine because it *looks* normal, but what Emily really needed to do was find ways to move ahead.

"What is something that brings you a lot of joy?" I asked her. Fresh flowers was the answer, no hesitation. Emily had always loved arranging colorful blooms in her kitchen. Whether a bouquet was an extra perk from a grocery run or cut from her carefully tended flower beds, their natural beauty never failed to give her a little boost in passing.

"Let's bring that joy into this space for you too," I told Emily. "Let's make it so your beautiful flowers are the first thing to greet you as you wake up every morning."

While organizing her kitchen cabinets, we came across a gorgeous vase that she had rarely let herself use. That vase now graces her bathroom vanity and almost always holds fresh blooms. When she's ready to fill the new drawers, I know she will—and in the meantime, she uses the flowers as a small but sweet reminder that there is beauty to be found, she is worth it, and it's going to be okay.

CONSUMER CULTURE

What is behind the knee-jerk tendency to keep our homes and lives filled to the brim, to constantly acquire? It's an appetite that's been fed by many sources over many decades.

The prosperity of the roaring twenties marked the beginning of American consumerism, and—if you think about it—that means that anyone reading this book has probably never lived through a time, at least in the United States, when the role of purchasing power wasn't tied into "the pursuit of happiness." And if pursuing social well-being through material goods wasn't enough of a motivator, we've also been encouraged by politicians to spend as a way of boosting the economy. It's patriotic.

Then there's the elephant in the room: the advertising industry with its megafunded psychological studies, working 24-7 to find new ways of telling our brains that we need more. Nothing like a "limited-time offer" to trigger the fear of missing out. In 2019, more than $240 billion were spent on advertising in the United States alone.[1] That doesn't include spending on social media and its *influencers*, personalities that will likely have more sway over what the next generation will consume than will any traditional marketing sources.

All together, that is a LOT of noise rumbling in our subconscious and reinforcing messages about what we need to acquire to be happy and to live better. But do strangers or a marketing machine *really* know what's best for your one-of-a-kind life? Or do you? With all that racket, it can be awfully hard to hear that inner voice, that innermost part of yourself that is always ready to communicate what it really needs to thrive if we listen with intention.

FILLING THE VOID SO WE DON'T FEEL THE VOID

Maybe it wouldn't be so hard to swim against the cultural current if the messages influencing our relationship to stuff were only external. But it also just *feels good* to purchase things. Literally. The moment we decide to buy, our brains get a hit of adrenaline and our bodies experience a rush of positive emotion. Even walking into a favorite store or logging on to a favorite shopping website is enough to trigger the release of dopamine in our brains. But like every type of high, there's a letdown afterward. And that's what keeps us going back for more.

When we're hooked into that cycle, shopping can become more about the buzz from acquiring the stuff than actually having (much less using) it. I have been guilty of this too—of buying to buy. And with anything you can imagine being available online, delivered instantly with the click of a button, it's so insanely easy to go with a whim, rather than think it through.

1 A. Guttmann, "U.S. Advertising Industry - Statistics & Facts," *Statista*, January 18, 2021, https:// www.statista.com/topics/979/advertising-in-the-us/.

I've done it. I've been there. I'm with you. Over the years, though, my work has caused me to examine my own purchasing habits more closely. And these days I realize how little I really need to be happy.

What does an unhealthy relationship with shopping look like? Some of the red flags might be:

- clothes on hangers with the tags still on them
- shopping bags or Amazon boxes lining the closet floor or entryway with the purchases still inside
- an inability to resist the lure of a "sale" even if you're not looking for anything in particular
- excessive credit card debt
- a constant yo-yo between "retail therapy" and buyer's remorse

No, I'm not against shopping. I'm actually all for acquiring things that add value and joy to your life—take Emily's flowers, for example. Yours truly can get just as much simple joy out of an iced-latte treat or some great nighttime facial cream as the next person. It's okay and natural to buy stuff that makes you feel good. But if you begin to make purchases in order *to not feel bad*, that's a problem. You may be masking (and not meeting) another very real need. The temporary mood-lifts may be keeping you from feeling something important—an area of your life that needs your care. Maybe it's a hurt relationship. A sense of failure in a certain area. Loneliness. Comparison. Grief. Not feeling like you're enough. If we're numb to the real needs in our lives, we'll never know how to heal, mend ourselves, and become happier and more whole. In fact, we won't know ourselves very well, in general.

Sometimes, unease with empty spaces or stillness can be a signal that we have work to do to become more at home within ourselves. But the very fact that you're choosing to read this book means you're already on the path to remedy that. By committing to thoroughly work through the contents of your home, you've already kicked off one heck of a self-discovery process.

WHEN THE BEST THINGS IN LIFE ARE FREE

Sometimes reconnecting with ourselves and establishing a healthier relationship to purchasing and possessions is simply about slowing down and making room in our hustle for simple activities and life-giving moments. Shifting down a gear can help bring clarity to what really makes you tick, makes you feel good, or brings you joy *outside of* the physical stuff.

Here's a little exercise that can help. Find an activity that you enjoy that doesn't involve acquiring any new possessions, or—an even better challenge—that doesn't involve spending money at all. For me, there's nothing like time outdoors to ground myself. I need those deep breaths in the open air. But this practice in finding simple gratification could look like anything that rejuvenates you or brings you (or someone else!) joy:

- hiking the trails near your home
- taking your pup to a dog park and watching him or her play
- hunting through that game cabinet and pulling out a long-lost puzzle or game for a fun night with friends or family
- reading a book on your shelf that you've always intended to read but never actually have
- scheduling a monthly coffee-on-the-back-porch date with a good friend
- doing YouTube yoga videos in your living room

- turning up the music for a kitchen dance party
- going for a drive, rolling down all the windows, and blasting your favorite song
- getting a buddy to volunteer a few hours a month with you at a local charity
- spreading a blanket in the grass at the park and picking shapes out of the clouds
- surprising your neighbor with a fresh batch of cookies

Like anything new, a simpler, slower-paced way of engaging in leisure time might feel a little awkward at first. But if you keep it up, soon you'll begin to feel more at peace with the practice, which in turn will enhance your life. And I bet you'll learn some things about yourself along the way too. Who knows, maybe you're a card shark, or maybe that afternoon drive through your neighborhood will allow you to notice things you never did before.

I love the freedom found in discovering that many of the things that add value to your lives are, well, (monetarily) free. And, with a little creativity and willingness to hunt, those things can include physical items too.

When helping Emily with her home, I knew that the job was about so much more than purging items and rearranging rooms; it was about re-imagining her life and the kids' lives in their space, and as a new kind of family. For years, Emily had talked about turning the garage into a family game room, with a ping-pong table as the main attraction. With one less car to pull in and a lot less clutter taking up space, now was the time, I told her, to fulfill this dream for the kids. Knowing her budget constraints, my team and I hunted down a great gently used ping-pong table that another family was giving away. On the last day of organizing their home, we set the table up in their transformed garage, and Emily surprised the kids after school.

Their pure excitement was just so sweet to witness.

I like imagining the kids and Emily in their new garage game room, laughing and connecting and crowning the latest victor of whatever family pursuit they can dream up. It reminds me that, when we make space for what we really need, sometimes even a hand-me-down ping-pong table can look like hope that the best is *still* yet to be.

BECOMING MORE "AT HOME" WITHIN OURSELVES

What I love most about true home-organizing work (not *tidying*) is that it's anything but surface level. Whenever we dig into the contents of our homes and actually try to understand what we've accumulated and why, we're really digging into the contents of our inner lives. That means that every mental or emotional barrier you may encounter while organizing your home has the potential to teach you something about yourself.

Sometimes just identifying a barrier that's particularly sticky for you can be freeing—just the awareness could help bring a perspective shift that leads to a breakthrough. But the exploration can also unearth some bigger issues that you many need extra support in navigating. Why do I keep getting stuck on this? Why can't I let go of these things? Is there a wound here that I haven't addressed? Where do I need closure? What barriers are blocking new growth and creativity in my life? Whatever questions may arise for you in the process—however big or insignificant they might feel—talking with a counselor can be invaluable for gaining insight.

Sound heavy-duty? It's actually the opposite. With every layer that's lifted, whether internal or external, you're going to become lighter. You'll be even more equipped to make space for what matters most in your life. And I genuinely hope that includes knowing and caring for yourself more deeply.

Remember when I said that I've learned that it actually takes very few things for me to be happy? Well, I'm still learning about myself. Aren't we always? But here's what I have discovered to be true so far: all it takes for me to love my life is (1) to work with deep purpose; (2) to live wholeheartedly (which I know I'm doing if I find myself laughing a lot, even if it's just at myself); and, most of all, (3) to give and receive love from the little tribe of people who know me best, soaking up quality time with them often as I can. Okay, okay. Throw in some good food, wine, and a patio, and I won't be mad about it. But that's really it. When those three main things are lit up, I feel such deep contentment. And you know what I find so encouraging? Everything on that list comes from within.

If no one's told you lately, it would be my honor to be the person to remind you that what you already have within you—what you're made of, what you've been created to do, your own brand of quirkiness, the way you find joy and give joy to the world—is enough to light up your own life too. No extra stuff required (okay, fine, maybe a ping-pong table).

before you begin

So now you've answered some of the big questions about what you want from your home, and you've identified some of the emotional barriers you might be up against as you begin the process of truly making your home your own.

As you roll up your sleeves and get ready to begin the tangible work of transforming your home one area at a time, there are a few simple things I want you to do before you dig into the process. Life is demanding, delightful, distracting, and precious all at once, and anytime we introduce a new, significant effort in the midst of our normal roll, things can get a little dicey. My hope is that these small actions can help shore up your head and heart, so that when life *does* knock you off the track toward creating a more life-giving home atmosphere, you can take a deep breath, take in some encouragement, and then find the way back to your course.

KEEP YOUR GOAL
WHERE YOU CAN SEE IT

Remember how, at the beginning of this book, I asked you directly: *What do you really want for your home?* Go back to that question and maybe this time get a little more specific with your answer. Ground it. Put real feet to it. Maybe you're saying: "I just want to send my kids off to school more peacefully every morning because we could find everything we needed, and I was able to be less frazzled and more present." Perhaps, like so many others in the workforce, you're now working remotely from home, so your goal centers around that: "I want my home office space to feel inspirational and free of all the distracting clutter. My goal is to create an environment where I actually want to sit down and engage in my work."

Whatever the key goal for your home looks like, write it down and put it somewhere you'll see it regularly. Stick it to the bathroom mirror, to the dashboard of your car, inside your planner, or on the door of your fridge. You could even make the goal a daily reminder on your phone. Let that note—wherever you place it—serve as a reminder of what you're working toward, a declaration that *this* outcome is going to be so worth the process.

DO A WALK-THROUGH OF YOUR HOME

In the next chapter I'm going to walk you through the foundational steps of the Life in Jeneral organizing method, which can be applied to any room or space of your home. But before tackling your first area, grab a notepad or open a note-taking app on your phone and do a walk-through of your entire dwelling. Room by room, take down a few notes of organizational challenges or goals in each space. I want you to rank the "pain level" you feel around the disorganization in that room or space from zero to ten: Zero is *I love being in this space. It has been purged of clutter and fully organized; every item in this space has a specific home.* Ten is *This space is such a problem that it gives me anxiety and keeps me up at night.*

Almost everyone has at least one key pain point in their home, if not several. It may not be visible from your curb, but it's always on the back of your mind—that guest room that still has boxes in it from your move three years ago, the bathroom cabinet crammed so full that something falls out every time you open it. Or you may just have the general sense that the aggressively colorful toys scattered on every surface of your home have secretly banded together to take over your life. Acknowledging the pain point directly and making a practical plan to address it can bring some initial mental relief, even if it's not the first space you can or should tackle when organizing your home.

MAKE A PRACTICAL PLAN
THAT FITS YOUR LIFESTYLE

Your work schedule, family situation, and any caregiving responsibilities are all going to play a role in how you're able to commit time to the process of organizing your home. It's up to you to decide what works best with your household's rhythm and routine. If you have vacation time and no kids at home, you may want to do an all-out blitz and knock out your entire home in a couple of weeks. Or maybe the most workable schedule for you is to block out two weekends a month and gradually work your way through your home, space by space, over the next six months. Whatever your plan, make it realistic for your lifestyle and needs and physically write your organizing schedule into your planner or onto the family calendar.

You might be wondering *Where should I start?* or *What order is best for tackling the rooms in my home?* I have a few rules of thumb to consider when deciding how to order your home-organizing plan:

- Never start with your home office (and paper-filing) or your garage. The types and amount of clutter these two spaces tend to attract typically take more time and energy to work through. It's too easy to get bogged down, distracted, and overwhelmed by starting in these spaces. I've seen it derail organizing efforts one too many times. Whatever rooms you store them in, save paper files, memorabilia, and photo organization for very last.
- Start with a small victory or two. Small spaces like a cleaning-supply closet, spice cabinet, or joy (versus junk!) drawers are great spots to gain confidence and momentum in the process. Plus, checking a few quick wins off the list is just so fun and energizing.
- Prioritize the spaces with the highest-ranking pain points in your home, *unless* they are the home office, paper files, or garage. (Just trust me on this!)

RALLY THE HOME TEAM

At Life in Jeneral, when we come into clients' homes, we're not only doing the physical work of organizing, we also serve as the emotional-support team and cheer squad for every client when they hit a snag or the process gets overwhelming. You need a support system too. This process takes a lot of energy and perseverance. Communicate with your household, not only on what you'll be doing but also on the big-picture purpose behind it. I hope you'll have lots of helping hands all throughout the process, but—on a very practical level—you may need assistance removing contents of rooms or lifting heavier items, especially in spaces like the garage.

Before you begin organizing, call on a bestie or sibling who can be your hype person, providing needed encouragement and decision-making help along the way. Pick someone who will be supportive but tell you the truth when you're waffling—someone who can catch and support this vision for your life and home.

Once you've opened your heart and completed those actions, it's time to get started.

PART 2

the
process

the life in jeneral method

STREAMLINE ANY SPACE WITH THESE
FOUNDATIONAL STEPS.

Now that you're getting down to it, here's something to remember when you're in the thick of organizing any space: the mess gets worse before it gets better. Yes, the outcome is going to be awesome, but don't freak out when—especially during the sorting and purging phases—it looks like a bomb went off and STUFF is everywhere. Don't let yourself get overwhelmed by it. Just keep going. I know you don't often see the messy side of professional organizing in all the Instagram-worthy posts, but even for professional crews, the scene can *look* like more madness than method. That's just part of the process.

The key is that there needs to be some method within the madness. Organizing or decluttering without a method means that you are more likely to get overwhelmed, and then to feel either like you have to hold on to everything in your home (you don't!) or that you should give up entirely (you shouldn't!).

When my team is working in a home, "the mess" is actually very strategic. Basically, we are following our five-step method, which is the secret to the Life in Jeneral organizing process. Since the various parts of your home will hold different kinds of significance, the soul work leading up to the method allows you to really figure out how each space can serve your home and the person you want to be there. And then this approach makes it easy to actually make that organization happen!

As we move from room to room in the following chapters, you'll see I focus most specifically on the areas of the home where I see my clients struggle with the heaviest accumulations of clutter, and the spaces where those mental and emotional barriers tend to surface most often. And while you won't see a chapter specifically dedicated to common living spaces—which take limitless forms depending on the home—it's important to note that the process you'll learn in the following Life in Jeneral method is designed to work in any and every kind of space in your home.

REMOVE ALL CONTENTS FROM THE SPACE

Take each and every item out of the space you are organizing. All shelves, cabinets, and drawers should be bare so you are starting with a clean slate.

Believe me, it can be tempting to cut corners on this step. And I get that. It feels like a lot of work to take out every little object, but it's vital to the success of the process. Being able to assess your full inventory in any given space is the key to being able to make fully informed decisions about what stays or goes. In a closet, for example, you'll be forced to look at those knitted sweaters from Aunt Suzy (seriously, what are those still doing there?). In your kitchen, you might find a wealth of expired goods or unused kitchen tools. Think about it this way: you can't know what isn't serving you if you can't see *everything*.

Once everything is out of the space, wipe down all shelves, drawers, and surfaces. A fresh, clean space is the foundation for the finished product.

CATEGORIZE AND SORT

In the next several chapters, you'll see the terms *zones* and *categories* often because those are the umbrellas under which you'll group your items. A zone is made up of related categories and categories are made up of similar, individual items. (For example, one zone in your pantry might be *breakfast items,* and the categories under *breakfast items* might be *cold cereals*, *hot cereals*, *breakfast bars*, and so forth.)

For each space you organize, you'll identify the zones and categories specific to your inventory in a space, and sort accordingly. This means you group all like items together so you can see how many of each item you have and where you may need to fill in some gaps. This step is where you really begin to understand the full scope of what you own or what you have accumulated in a space. So in a closet, you'd be putting dresses in one piles, shoes in another, etc.

STEP THREE

DISCARD AND DONATE

When you have removed all the items from the space and sorted them into categories, it's time to decide what to *discard* (recycling anything you can and tossing what you can't) or *donate* (giving away anything in good repair that someone else could use). This step, which I sometimes call *purging*, is where those mental and emotional barriers to organizing are most often triggered. But asking yourself the right questions (and answering honestly) can really help.

Ask yourself these questions when working through clutter in any room of the home:

- Do I love it, use it, or need it?
- Do I have duplicates?
- Is it broken beyond repair?
- Does it belong to me? (If borrowed, it's probably time to give it back!)
- Would I want it if I didn't already have it? (Tip: Look up the *psychology of ownership* or the *endowment effect*.)
- Is it expired?
- Would I buy it again?

- Am I saving it for someone else?
- Do I have the space for this where I live today?
- If it hadn't been brought to my attention, would I even have missed it?
- Is it serving the lifestyle I want to create?
- Is it critical to save? If so, why? (The answer to *why* should serve your life in the present.)

It's okay if this step in the process takes some time—that's totally normal. Emotional barriers often resurface during the purge, making you question why you'd get rid of *anything* to begin with. If you're getting overwhelmed while going through the questions, I recommend taking a break. Make a cup of coffee, or go for a walk, and while you're doing so envision the home you want to live in. Getting your mindset back to the big picture will give you the reset you need to keep going. When you get back to the process, you'll be doing so with fresh eyes.

STEP FOUR
ADD ORGANIZATIONAL SYSTEMS

When you've worked through what you're going to keep and you've removed what will be discarded or donated, you'll know how much stuff you actually need to store. You can begin determining where to place each zone in the space and what kind of organizational system will work best for both the space and the items stored there.

An organizational system is a system created to separate and hold categories of items. Adding containers ensures that every item in a space has a specific home that can be maintained as you move through life. You're going to learn a lot about containment and labeling in the following chapters, and that's because both are essential to long-term success for any system.

Containers! This is where all the fun comes in: bins, baskets, trays, carts, drawer dividers, and more—of all sizes, shapes, and styles. There are seemingly endless options for organizing products and—even for professionals—it takes a little trial and error to find the right container that fits a specific space and fits the type of inventory being stored.

My recommendation is to overbuy a little bit on product types so that—once you've purged and are ready to place items back in a space—you can "puzzle-piece" various containers into the actual drawer, shelf, or cabinet to see what fits best with both your aesthetic and size of the space. Keep your receipts and return excess after organizing! You really won't know what works best until you're hands-on in the space trying things out. So give yourself the flexibility to experiment and have fun with it!

Some of the most frequent questions we get asked at Life in Jeneral are about what kind of products to use for containing. Visit *www.lifeinjeneral.com* to see our current favorites and where we source them.

Even if you have zero budget for products, though, *please* don't let that slow you down when it comes to getting your home organized. Shoeboxes or Tupperware will work, too! Most of the products will be stored inside other spaces—like closets, pantries, etc.—and won't be immediately visible in your home anyway, so prioritize functionality at this juncture. Remember, you can always go back and replace the actual containers down the line.

A NOTE ON STYLING YOUR SPACES

If you do decide to style from the get-go, there's good news: with so many textures and styles of bins, baskets, and containers available, you'll be able to add a personal design aesthetic to any space you're organizing. Here's my philosophy when it comes to styling: you can marry beauty with function, but function must win in the end.

Yes, function is queen, but here's why aesthetics matter too: if you find beauty in the way a space is set up in your home, and if you feel inspired when you enter that area, you are *so* much more likely to respect it. And treating a space with respect means putting things back thoughtfully rather than haphazardly. So, however you choose to style your spaces, do it in such a way that it feels beautiful and inspirational to you. Because you will be much more motivated to keep it that way.

STEP FIVE

MAINTAIN

Once each item and each category has a home, you will always know where to return them when done with use. When organizational systems are in place, it's really not hard to maintain them, but it does require commitment. Small daily habits make all the difference. *(We'll talk more about maintaining your organized home in chapter 17.)*

SUPPLIES TO GET STARTED

So now that you're getting down to it, what do you need on hand to get going? Really, not much! Here's what I'd recommend having on hand:

- *trash bags* (for collecting and carting off discard, donate, or recycle piles)
- *large bins* or *boxes* (to separate items that you're sorting into categories), or
- *blue painter's tape* and a *Sharpie marker* (to mark off zones on the floor for sorting items or to use in place of sticky notes for identifying zones in a space before you put items back)
- *a label maker* (doesn't have to be fancy!) or *paint/chalk pens* (for labeling)

If you have a low-traffic room, like a home office or guest room, it's nice to have a staging area—a designated space to temporarily spread out your project—that's not in the middle of a busy family room as you work to pull out and sort items from a space, especially if organizing that space requires more than one day.

Another thing I recommend is scheduling breaks. Like I said earlier, taking a walk or a few minutes to call a friend can be helpful! And if that friend is part of the crew motivating you, they might even be able to weigh in on places where you're really struggling and give some clarity on those items. The key is to remove the pressure from the situation however possible. Set yourself up to win.

And I can't emphasize this enough: don't let anything—lack of supplies, products, time, or staging space—keep you from simply *starting*. You can do this. You now have all the tools.

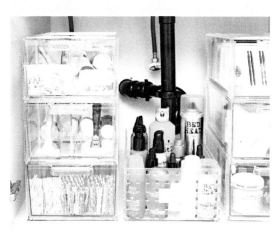

bathroom

CREATE A SMOOTHER START AND END TO YOUR DAY
WITH A STREAMLINED SPACE FOR SELF-CARE.

The bathroom is often overlooked when it comes to home organization—we don't spend a lot of concentrated time there and tend to underestimate the amount of products housed in what can be one of the smaller rooms of a home. Yet it's also one of the most frequently used areas of the home. It's typically the first stop upon waking and the last stop before bed. And moments spent here, no matter how brief, can have a significant impact on how we feel not only about our home, but about our days and nights in general. There are simple factors that play into this, the biggest one being that most people don't actually have bathrooms that are optimized for their lifestyle.

As you go into your bathroom, ask whether the set-up and supplies are in sync with your lifestyle. Does the room set the stage for a smooth start and peaceful close to the day? It should. And once you streamline the products and tools that support your daily routine, it definitely will.

COMMON PROBLEMS

The bathroom typically houses a majority of your health, hygiene, beauty, and skincare products. That amounts to a lot of small items and products in one limited space. Outside of taking a good soak in the tub, people don't linger for long periods of time in the bathroom, so in a place that feels hurried, it's easy to toss something you're not using in a drawer and plan to just come back later. But when does later actually come? Add the complexity and additional items that a (dare we say *messy*) partner or roommate can add to the drawers, cabinets, and countertops, and this space can seem more like an unmanageable little circus than a peaceful, efficient place to get ready for the day, transition for whatever's next, or wind down for bed. (Plus, there's always the added little emotional trigger if your significant other can't be bothered to squeeze the toothpaste tube from the bottom rather than the middle, right? Separate toothpaste tubes for all. Who's with me on this?!)

Needless to say, it's all too easy for the drawers and cabinets in this space to wind up resembling catch-all spaces, with no rhyme or reason to the contents inside. The key to avoiding a chronic mess here lies in getting real with what you actually use and need, creating categories specific to your inventory and proper containment for each. The most common challenges or pitfalls I see in this area are:

- a lack of storage space
- underutilized tall or deep storage spaces
- expired items
- nearly empty (or half-used and abandoned) product containers
- messy shelves (due to a lack of containment or bins)
- unrelated or unalike items in the same space without rhyme or reason
- duplicates
- overfilled drawers and cabinets
- cluttered counter spaces

HOW TO CATEGORIZE AND SORT

Despite having smaller square footage than most other rooms in a home, bathrooms pack an impressive amount of products in a small space. Once you've pulled everything out of your bathroom, you can begin to identify the larger categories that make up your bathroom's inventory and sort through your items, grouping like items together. Every home is different and you will likely need to create categories that are unique to your routine. Adapt or add to the categories listed below so that they work for you:

- face and skin care products
- hair care products
- oral care products
- medicines, vitamins, and supplements
- makeup
- travel products
- bath and shower products
- linens
- first aid
- heat tools for hair
- shaving products
- feminine care products

WHAT TO DISCARD AND DONATE

Before you begin the purging process, here are a few things to keep in mind to help you stay focused on honing your bathroom inventory to where it becomes a tool kit of products and tools that truly serve you in this space.

It can be hard to let go of skincare and beauty products in particular. First, there's the cost; they're expensive. But even free samples can tend to stick around longer than they should. Whether it's softer skin, less wrinkles, the perfect smoky eye, or more happiness in general, these types of products tend to make big promises. But here's the bottom line: if you didn't like the way it smelled, looked, or felt on your skin the first time you used it, you're not going to later on. The true purpose of these goods is to take extra good care of *yourself.* You are still in line with that goal if you cull your products down to what actually works for you and makes you feel good. The rest is clutter that's getting in the way of putting your best (calm, contented, and assured) self forward every morning.

KEEP IT CURRENT: CHECK ALL EXPIRATION DATES!

Hanging on to expired items is a huge sticking point in the bathroom especially. Sometimes it comes from a mindset of wondering what the harm is of keeping it; other times, you might hold on to an expired tube of lipstick as a reminder to buy another. But when current products are mixed in with expired ones, the space doesn't function as well as it should.

It can be tempting to keep makeup that has expired, but remember the reasons it has an expiration date in the first place. Not only does the quality of the product break down, but makeup also collects bacteria over time that can cause breakouts on skin or other problems. And if a product isn't utilized often enough to be used up before expiring, maybe that tells you something too?

My advice is the same when it comes to medication: let go of everything that is expired or outdated. If you are giving yourself the care you deserve, you should be seeing your health professionals often enough to assess what you need *today*. And if you're not yet, it's not too late, but there's really no benefit to holding on to expired meds. As with makeup, their potency decreases over time, meaning that if you *do* need that type of medication down the line, the expired tubes you have won't do the job you need them to do.

Many items that take up space in the bathroom are duplicates, free samples, or items that were purchased once and have since been abandoned or forgotten. As you're working through your bathroom inventory, pause on each item and ask yourself:

* Do I currently use this product?
* Is this part of my regular routine?
* Do I actually need this?
* Why did I buy this in the first place?

From personal hygiene to first aid supplies, remember that anything unopened and unexpired can be donated to women's or family shelters.

ADDING ORGANIZATIONAL
SYSTEMS

Whatever space you're working with, your goal is to tailor the organizational systems within it to fit your particular lifestyle. When I'm helping a client organize their bathroom, I always have them walk me through their daily routines step by step. Everyone's process is different. But whether it takes you ten steps and ten products to get ready for the day, or just two steps and some toothpaste, your daily-use items are the ones that should be most accessible in your space, and you should work down the list from there.

general guidelines
FOR PLACEMENT IN THE BATHROOM

Once you've pared back your bathroom inventory to only the things that best power up and power down your days, it's time to find the right homes for your newly categorized items. Tailor your zones to fit your particular needs, and use these lists simply as a general guide:

IN CABINETS OR ON SHELVES

- linens and towels
- shampoos and conditioners

- medicines
- tall bottles and jars
- makeup bags

- lotions
- perfumes

IN BASKETS AND BINS

- small towels
- bath soaps

- face washes
- toilet paper

- stockpiled products

IN SHALLOW DRAWERS

- toothpastes
- toothbrushes

- cotton products
- shaving products

- makeup
- hair ties and accessories

IN DEEP DRAWERS

- hot hair tools
- toilet paper

- tall bottles and jars
- face washes

- bulky gadgets

ON THE COUNTERTOP

- hand soap

- a toothbrush holder

- diffusers

space-saving tips
IN THE BATHROOM

If you're tight on space in your bathroom, staying organized can seem especially challenging. How can you create systems when there's not enough storage space to keep items in the same categories together? Luckily, there are plenty of tricks and tools to make the most of any set up. If your bathroom lacks drawer or cabinet capacity, consider these methods.

"UNBOXING" ITEMS AND DISCARDING PACKAGING

Remove as many toiletry items as you can from their original packaging (cotton balls, cotton swabs, tampons, etc.). Typically, packaging is bulky and takes up prime real estate, especially in a tight space.

UTILIZE THE BACK OF THE DOOR

Over-the-door storage units are one of my favorite systems to implement in a small space like a bathroom. If your bathroom lacks the drawer and cabinet space you need, consider using a hanging unit to store anything from hair tools and accessories to bath products and backstock. Depending on your needs, the storage baskets for these units come in different sizes. Grab the larger baskets for bulky shampoo and conditioner bottles, for example, or a smaller version if you just need a place to stash your makeup and accessories.

USING A CART

Similar to the over-the-door storage hack, using a rack on wheels is another great solution for those of you who lack overall space in your bathroom. A cart that can be easily moved makes it simple to shift objects around if you need more storage but have a tight space.

USING SHALLOW DRAWERS EFFECTIVELY

Store

* *General daily-use items.* Whatever you incorporate into your everyday routine (e.g., toothpaste, toothbrush, floss, Q-tips, etc.) should be closest at hand.
* *Everyday makeup.* You'll want your everyday makeup in an easy-to-pull-from location. And since most makeup products come in smaller containers, you can maximize shallow drawer space.

Use

* *Acrylic drawer organizers.* Using clear organizers gives your drawer a clean look and eliminates all of the clutter that comes with original product packaging.
* *Modular bins.* Using bins of different sizes gives you the ability to mix and match based on item size. It's okay to put a variety of items into one bin as long as they belong to the same category.

USING DEEP DRAWERS EFFECTIVELY

Store

* *Bulky stuff.* This could include blow-dryers, curling irons, hairbrushes, and more. Bathroom items are better suited for deep drawers than shallow drawers, because they require different types of storage bins and containers.

Use

* *Deep drawer dividers.* Along with bulky items and tools that require more space, deep drawers are great for products that tend to come in taller containers, like aerosol hair sprays.
* *Deep drawer bins.* Compartmentalize with deep drawer bins or deep bins with dividers. There are tons of different types of bins to choose from. Whether you decide based on your preferred aesthetic or are focused on function, remember to measure the depth of your drawer so the bin does not exceed the drawer height.

sheltie organization

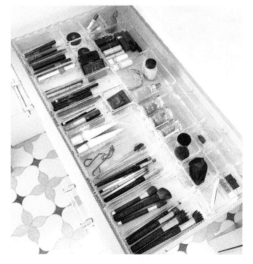

contain to maintain

USING CABINETS AND SHELVES EFFECTIVELY

Use

- *Lazy Susans.* When it comes to multiple items together in bathroom cabinets and shelves, things can easily get lost. Lazy Susans—rotating, circular trays—are my go-to solution for being able to see and access anything quickly. With these spinning wheels, nothing is ever hidden in the back row. Whether it be for hair products, backstock items, or lotions, this is a containment solution I come back to again and again.

- *Baskets for linens.* Storing your hand towels and other bathroom linens in baskets on an open shelf makes for a clean look and can be a nice way to break up all of the bins and containers, adding a simple yet decorative flair to your spaces. With so many textures and materials to choose from, baskets are a fun way to add in your personal style in a space that can otherwise feel heavily utilitarian.

USING THE SPACE UNDER THE SINK EFFECTIVELY

Store

- Bulky piping under the bathroom sink can make this space feel difficult to make the most of. But I find that it's often underestimated and underutilized for storage. Because under-the-sink cabinets are typically on the taller side for plumbing, they can be actually great for storing taller products (like large shampoo, conditioner, and hairspray bottles) that don't fit on shelves elsewhere. Use that vertical space to your advantage! Use stackable drawers with drawer dividers to create lasting and maintainable systems for items you don't use every day, like backstock, heat tools for hair, and travel-size toiletries.

MAKING IT YOURS

Now for the fun part! You likely have some extra bathroom items that don't quite fit into any of your new bathroom systems. Whether it's bath salts, perfumes, or scented candles, a few small decorative items can add a touch of countertop flair. The key is to decorate your counter with a few accent pieces without overfilling the space or infringing on functionality.

If your lifestyle works best when your daily routine items are out on the counter, implement a solution that complements your natural flow, such as acrylic counter organizers to store your makeup and/or daily products. Bottom line: make this process work for you. There are always multiple organizing solutions for one space, and as I tell my clients, organizing isn't a one-size-fits-all kind of deal.

With a little creativity, a spatial challenge in a room is an opportunity to marry beauty and function. And it gives me such a kick when the resulting solution ends up being my client's favorite part of the space. One memory that brings me a lot of joy has to do with a makeup cart (of all things!) that my team and I put together for my client, Jan. To make Jan's bathroom sink accessible with her wheelchair, it sits lower than a standard sink with no cabinet or storage underneath. That made Jan's morning routine literally tough to maneuver because it was difficult for her to reach any beauty or hygiene items when sitting at the sink. So we sourced a small but gorgeous acrylic rolling cart and arranged all of Jan's beauty inventory in this one mobile unit that slipped neatly into the nook beside her sink and mirror. Everything she needed to get ready for the day was now in arm's reach. But utility wasn't all we were going for. That little tray on wheels had extra swag, with its chrome top tray and trim and clear swivel wheels, because I wanted the presentation of the cart itself to make Jan feel beautiful. The glowing grin on her face when she first laid eyes on it was all the confirmation I needed that we had hit the mark.

primary closet and bedroom

CURATE A SPACE THAT INSPIRES
A DAILY DOSE OF CONFIDENCE.

When you enter your closet area every morning, can you quickly find what you need? Do you feel good about everything you pull out to wear or use?

If not, your closet is not serving your life like it could and should be. You should not have to spend precious time and energy rummaging through piles and yanking on tangled hangers every morning just to walk out the door in something you're second-guessing all day long. Yet that's what many of my clients are doing on a daily basis before we remake their closet space. What a distraction from your day and, well, your life!

Closets are a tricky space to organize. Not only are there lots of categories in a wardrobe that can accumulate excess, but seasons change, fashion trends come and go, and so do personal tastes. Clothing can also hold sentimental value; whether it's a dress you wore to your best friend's wedding, or a beloved sweater that belonged to a family member, I get why those pieces matter. I want them to shine, too.

That's why I want to help you streamline the flow of your closet by creating designated zones for all of your clothing items and accessories, determining the best way to store them, and establishing lasting systems that you can maintain. I want you to know what you have, know that everything you own fits and is flattering to your body, and know where to find it all. That's a lot of *knowing*—and that in itself is a confidence booster. And I don't care if your power suit is a sweatshirt and yoga pants, there's no better way to put your best foot forward than with confidence.

COMMON PROBLEMS

Whether you have a small closet with limited storage or a walk-in with an abundance of breathing room, the two major factors contributing to a hot-mess closet tend to be the same across the board: (1) people don't like the actual space, how the closet's arranged (or isn't)—they don't know how to make their particular space work for their own clothes, accessories, and other storage—and (2) they don't love or feel confident about what's *in* their closet.

As a result, here's what tends to manifest:

- overcrowded clothing rods
- overflow of items
- piles of garments building up on the floor
- wrinkled items
- tangled hanging clothes
- an inability to find things
- inadequate storage for accessories
- messy shelves
- items that don't suit your lifestyle

how to
CATEGORIZE AND SORT

The good news is that once you can actually see and really understand all of your closet's inventory, half the battle is won. When you've pulled everything out of your closet—and before you begin deciding what stays or goes—begin sorting your items into the categories below. Compiling one category completely (so that every sweater you own is together, then every pair of jeans you own is together, etc.) before moving on to the next will keep you focused and help you avoid getting overwhelmed by the inevitable messiness of this part of the process.

CLOTHES THAT ARE HUNG
Categorize and sort your hanging tops, pants, skirts, dresses, jeans, jackets, and sweaters. Sort anything that lives in the closet into like item categories.

Sweaters

Depending on the material, some of your sweaters are better stored by keeping them folded on a shelf or in a drawer, while others can be safely hung (see "Sweater Care: To Hang or Not to Hang?" on page 142).

Jeans

If you hang your jeans, you may have already put these together in a pile. Sort them by color and style (e.g., low-rise, high-rise, skinny jean, etc.).

CLOTHES THAT ARE FOLDED AND IN DRAWERS

Remove everything from your drawers and sort into tops, bottoms, intimates and undergarments, pajamas, athletic wear, swimwear, etc.

BAGS AND PURSES

Sort bags and purses by size or occasion, whichever is more suitable to your lifestyle.

SHOES

Sort shoes based on type (e.g., sandals, sneakers, boots, heels, etc.)

ACCESSORIES AND JEWELRY

This category includes scarves, hats, jewelry, ties, etc. Categorize and sort into piles.

DONATING, DISCARDING, AND SELLING

Before you sift through your closet categories to decide what stays or goes, I want you to sit with this exhortation for a minute: *commit to the present*. What best serves you and your life *today*? You've already seen that answering this question is central to successful organizing in any area of the home, but I can't overemphasize how key that commitment is when you're making decisions as personal as your clothing choices.

In almost every home I work in, I find a section of clothes in the closet that are being saved for *someday*. For when my client loses those five, ten, or fifty pounds someday. I find the jeans that haven't been worn in ten years, but *this year*, my client tells me, they'll do all the right things and fit back into them.

Friend, I am *all* for you being the healthiest version of your body, mind, and soul—whatever that looks like for you. But let me tell you, staring at perceived shame or failure every day in the form of ill-fitting clothes taking up prime real estate in your closet is *not* the way to become a healthier you. Be honest—has it served you in a sustainable way so far, or does it wind up making you just feel kind of bummed to look at piles of clothes you like but aren't wearing? I think a lot of people feel that holding on to those clothes *is* a motivator, and I'm here to say that usually that isn't the case. Usually those clothes wind up making you feel less than, and you aren't.

Here is your challenge: honor who and where you are today with what you choose to keep in your closet. That act of faith, that soul work of choosing to celebrate yourself now (instead of conditionally, in the future, *if and when* you one day meet that goal) will produce more positive long-term results than you can imagine.

Wanna know something crazy? Many of my clients who make the conscious decision to finally let those "one day" clothes go end up losing the weight or achieving that long-held health goal in the months that follow. I can't put stats around it, but I've witnessed it. I've witnessed my clients free themselves by getting rid of unhealthy "motivators" that are in reality having the opposite effect.

Honor where you are today. Show yourself kindness in how you choose to fill up your present. And trust that tomorrow will be better for it. Because it will be.

Questions to Ask as You Work Through Your Closet

- Do I love it, wear it, and feel good in it?
- Does this outfit fit my current body type?
- Does this represent something I would feel proud of and confident to be seen in?
- Does this fit my current lifestyle?
- When was the last time I wore this?
- Do I need multiple of these?
- Would I buy this again?

PHONE A FRIEND

When it comes to my own clothes, I know what feels good to me, but I don't always know what pieces *look* best on me. That's where a trusted friend with good taste can really come in handy. If you're the same way, consider asking a gentle but truthful friend with a good sense of fashion to help you determine which items are not only worth keeping, but are confidence-boosting staples. A fun way to do this is by having a mini fashion show. Pour your friend a glass of wine, turn up your favorite music, and try on all the items. You'll keep the pieces you love, and the ones you decide to toss or donate you'll be able to send off with a happy memory.

WHAT TO DISCARD VS. DONATE

If you're not sure whether something should be donated or just tossed from your closet space, here's what I suggest:

Discard

- ripped or torn items
- stained clothing
- stretched-out clothing
- discolored clothing
- shoes with holes
- shoes with broken straps

Donate

- unnecessary duplicates
- free T-shirts that you don't wear
- shoes that no longer fit
- shoes that are uncomfortable
- bridesmaids' dresses
- old work uniforms
- old costumes

Sell

If you have items of value that you'd rather sell than donate, there are a ton of online resources for that. Check *www.lifeinjeneral.com* for recommendations of great places to sell your clothing online. You can also see if there are consignment shops in your town that would take the pieces on.

MEMORIES

As I mentioned earlier, the closet is often a space where nostalgic or sentimental clothing or accessories that are no longer worn are stored. Whether this means your wedding dress, a loved one's sweater, or a childhood memento, if those items are really special to you, bring you joy, and you have space to keep them, don't hesitate to hold on to them. You should absolutely be keeping room for those items.

But in going through everything, keep in mind the emotional barriers. Are any of the items being stored out of guilt? Is there anything you don't want but feel you can't—or shouldn't—let go of?

When you take a thorough inventory, decide what is truly most important to you. Then place those items in their own container or bin of display, such as a memory box or bin. Finding a place for them and keeping them separate from your everyday things will ensure that you are more likely to remember and enjoy that you have them, as well as ensure the comfort of always knowing where they are. And by prioritizing the items that offer the most sentimental value, you're freeing yourself to let go of the ones that don't.

general guidelines FOR CLOTHING PLACEMENT

Okay, take a breath! You did the hard mental work of deciding what to purge—now it's time to have some fun putting this space together.

LIJ TIP: Before placing items back in your closet, use sticky notes or blue painter's tape to temporarily label what goes where and place them on your drawers and shelves. This makes it easier to determine how much space you have and it simplifies the process of putting everything back.

ON RODS

If your closet capacity doesn't allow for all of the items listed here to be hung, don't worry. Many of the items can live, folded, in other areas of the closet, as space allows:

- tops, blouses, and shirts
- jeans
- khakis

- trousers and dress pants
- skirts
- dresses

- jackets and heavy coats (on coat hangers)
- suits and tuxedos (on suit hangers)

ON SHELVES

With the proper containment, these items store well on shelves:

- shoes
- jeans
- sweatshirts

- sweaters
- hats
- purses

- jewelry

IN DRAWERS

Whether you have a dresser built into your closet space or in your room, here are the items that should be folded and placed in drawers:

- underwear and boxers
- socks

- athletic tops and bottoms

- pajamas
- swimwear

HOW TO HANG ITEMS PROPERLY

ARRANGE BY TYPE, FREQUENCY OF USE, AND COLOR

Since you've already gone through and categorized your clothing, it will be easy to arrange them in the closet with like items grouped together.

Place categories in the closet in accordance with how often you wear them. Everyday staples should go toward the front or in an easier-to-access area. Formal gowns and special-occasion attire should be placed farther back in less-frequented areas. Fill in the gaps in between to fit your lifestyle.

One tip I always suggest is color coordinating; doing this with your garments within each category (think rainbow order or ROYGBIV) can make for a beautiful, cohesive look. Arrange clothing within each category from light to dark, with lighter colors closer to the entrance of the closet space.

FACE CLOTHES THE SAME DIRECTION

Make sure all items of clothing are facing toward you so that they are easily visible and you can access them faster. This will also help your clothes hang more neatly and avoid getting snagged on each other.

HANG YOUR PANTS

To save more space and create a cleaner look, fold your pants in half lengthwise so the back pockets are visible and drape your pants over the hanger with the back inseam facing the wall of your closet. This method allows them to lay smoother and not wrinkle.

SWEATER CARE: TO HANG OR NOT TO HANG?

Typically, sweaters with zippers, or sweaters made of silk or any other material that might wrinkle, should be hung. Cashmere sweaters should be folded and put on shelves or in drawers or bins. For longevity, sweaters with a small neck or narrow shoulders should also be folded rather than hung to prevent being stretched out of shape.

Moths can be a significant issue if you live near the coast or any area with humidity. Use cedar planks or balls to protect your cashmere, wool, or silk sweaters behind closed doors or in bins.

closet organization

To protect the shape and prolong the life of your garments, make sure you're hanging your clothes with the appropriate type of hanger for each category of clothes: a shirt-and-sweater hanger, a skirt hanger, a suit-jacket hanger, or a pants hanger.

SPACE-SAVING TIPS: HANGING CLOTHES

I've found that many people simply put clothes on hangers and place them in the closet without rhyme or reason. The key to an organized and maintainable closet is creating the space to see—and easily pull out or replace—everything you own. You may not have the physical space to separate your clothes, but here are some tools to help in even the smallest of closets.

USE CLOSET ROD DIVIDERS

I love closet rod dividers as a way to maintain the zones or categories you have created for yourself. These space holders allow you to create a home for each type of clothing and create structure on a simple hanging rod.

SWITCH TO MATCHING HANGERS

You probably have a variety of mismatched hangers in your closet: some bulky, some flimsy (I see you, dry cleaner hangers!). Now is an ideal time to convert all of your hangers to the same kind. Not only does this dramatically improve the cohesive look of a closet, it helps save space. Slimline hangers are fantastic for saving space as they are flat and fit together, and don't tangle like wire hangers have a tendency to do. One caveat to the matching-hanger goal: for coats and suit jackets, you'll want the thicker wooden coat hangers to preserve the shape of the garments, especially in the shoulders.

COLOR COORDINATE

Color coordinating is a personal preference. Some people like to color co-ordinate their closets for aesthetic purposes, others because it's easier to access items. Overall, it's a great way to save time in your morning routine and also maintain categories on your rod. And yes, it looks *great*.

space-saving tips
IN DRAWERS

There's no better way to maximize the capacity of a single drawer than to divide it into multiple compartments, creating definitive spaces for each category. Make the most of your drawer space with these tips.

USE EXPANDABLE DRAWER DIVIDERS

After categorizing the contents of your drawer, you'll likely find that you have more categories than drawers. Enter expandable drawer dividers! These tools are essential to maintaining organization in almost any drawer. I've found them especially helpful for keeping clients from just tossing things into drawers; once those are delineated by space, it's harder to justify tossing pieces in randomly.

TRY FILE FOLDING

File folding is the number-one space-saving trick within the LIJ organizing method. With this technique, an article of clothing is folded into a com-pact rectangle so that it can stand upright in a drawer. Not only does this method maximize drawer space, it also allows you to see every clothing item in that drawer with just one glance. No more digging through layers of stacked clothing to find something! While it may seem like a challenge at first, with our tutorial video (which you can find at *www.lifeinjeneral.com*) and a little practice, you'll become a file-folding pro, and you'll be amazed at the amount of drawer space you didn't know you had. Seriously, this is a game changer!

USE MODULAR COMPARTMENTS

For accessories without an obvious home, consider utilizing modular drawer compartments. If you have a spare shallow drawer in your closet, these are especially great for storing things like ties, sunglasses, watches, etc.

space-saving tips
ON THE SHELVES

Oftentimes, shelves can be the trickiest places to maintain organization in a closet. It's too tempting to simply try to stack items on top of each other in a slippery heap, making it almost impossible to access objects from the pile without making a mess—sort of like Jenga for clothing items. But with the right kinds of containment in place, your closet shelves can actually become the easiest place to create and maintain structure for storing your things.

USE SWEATER BINS

Use stackable shirt-and-sweater bins to contain sweaters on shelves. If you don't have the space to hang your sweaters, or you want to keep the more delicate ones from stretching, these bins are a great way to save space on your rods while keeping your shelf organization crisp and clean.

USE BASKETS

Have fun picking stylish baskets for beanies, gloves, or any other smaller items that are not hung. I love the warmth and texture baskets bring to any space, the closet included.

USE SHELF DIVIDERS

It can be a challenge trying to make your small clutches or oddly shaped bags look nice on shelves, and an even bigger challenge to keep them arranged so that they're not stacked one on top of another. Acrylic dividers create the perfect-size slots to attractively display all of your bags, large and small.

USE BOXES AND BINS

To store any seasonal items you don't want to be visible, utilize bins and boxes on upper shelves. Just be sure to label each container so you know what's inside at a glance. These can be as simple as cardboard boxes labeled WINTER ACCESSORIES or SUMMER ACCESSORIES, but the key is to make sure that you know what's inside.

SHOE STORAGE

Whether you have built-in shoe storage, use over-the-door units, or are creating your own containment system with bins on shelves, the rule of thumb for placement is the same: keep the pairs you wear most often easily within reach and accessible. Here are some solutions for storing your shoes with intention.

CREATE A SHOE WALL

In whatever form it takes, whether it's built-in or a DIY wall of floating shelves or stackable shoe bins, a shoe wall is the backbone to an organized closet. Place the shoes that are worn most often in easy-to-reach places, and arrange less-frequented shoes on higher shelves. If your compartments are small, a good trick for getting the most out of the space is facing one shoe forward and one backward.

USE OVER-THE-DOOR SHOE STORAGE

If your closet is on the snug side, an over-the-door shoe-storage unit is a practical solution and great space-saver. And one big perk here is that the closet floor will then be clear.

USE SHOE BINS

Storing shoes in plastic bins is an effective way to preserve the longevity of your shoes—and it's a great way to protect them from dust, too. If you have room for this option, be sure to label each bin with the specific shoe type.

BOOT STORAGE

If you're like most of my clients, your tall boots end up randomly stashed in a closet corner because they don't fit in your shoe-storage area and they don't have a designated space. Here are some solutions for storing your boot collection with intention.

Hang Your Boots

If you have adjustable shelving in your built-ins, use a rod under the bottom shelf to hang your tall boots on hooks.

Use Boot Shapers

If you don't have adjustable built-ins that allow for boots, boot shapers will not only keep your boots standing upright on any shelf with enough height, they also serve to maintain your boots' form over time.

Use Boot Boxes

Alternatively, if you have a smaller closet space and don't have room to store seasonal boots in the open, utilize boot boxes. I particularly like the Container Store brand boot boxes.

JEWELRY STORAGE

When choosing how to store your jewelry, keep in mind your particular lifestyle and what role jewelry plays in it. Are you someone who puts the same pieces on every day? Is jewelry for special occasions only?

Personally, I wear very little jewelry and have only a small amount that is special to me, so a single jewelry tray with inserts in a closet drawer works perfectly for my purposes. Some of my clients enjoy collecting beautifully crafted jewelry as a type of artwork, so seeing it out and on display is almost as much fun for them as wearing it. I think that's a win-win. Totally depends on your lifestyle.

If you have a free surface in your closet and want to display your pieces, pretty trays on a dresser top might be your thing. If you wear jewelry daily and have an empty wall in your closet, you may want to hang pieces both for function and a little decorative flair. Or maybe you have really expensive jewelry and a locked drawer is the answer. Stackable jewelry trays are a popular option for keeping a larger quantity and variety of pieces contained and easy to access.

In other words, there's no wrong way to approach storing your jewelry, as long as each piece has its own little home and you can easily see and access what you need when you're inspired to wear it. What you don't want to happen is to be looking through a gym bag and finally find your favorite pair of earrings . . . five months after you needed them.

shoes

accessories

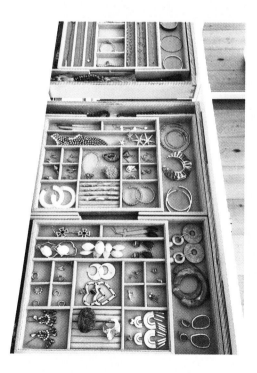

ACCESSORIES AND MISCELLANEOUS STORAGE

Closets are as unique as the individuals they belong to. If you have extra or miscellaneous items leftover after placing your main categories, use them to spice up your space. Try these solutions to organize and style your accessories.

HANG YOUR BAGS

Have extra wall space? Hang your bags using Command hooks. Extra room on your hanging rod? Try acrylic purse hangers or S-hooks.

PROP YOUR HATS

If hats are your thing, boost the playful or elegant tone by styling your space with hat props, or hang your hats on the wall using adhesive hooks or nails.

CREATE STORAGE SPACES FOR YOUR COLLECTIONS

Many people enjoy collecting fashion accessories. Whether it be eyeglasses, watches, pins, or whatever strikes your fancy, create a storage space for those items. Accessory organizers are available specifically for this purpose, or mix-and-matching modular compartments work great too.

DESIGNATE A PERFUME DRAWER

Extra drawer space, if you have it, is perfect for storing perfume backstock.

MAKING IT YOURS

Maybe you've never thought about a closet as an area that could benefit from styling or decor. But you don't have to be someone who gets excited about fashion to have a closet that inspires you. That's what's so fun and personal about it all—what lights you up is distinct, unique from anyone else. And the finishing touches in your home can reflect that.

GLAMMA'S GLOVES

My dear friend Valorie had a deeply special connection with her grand-mother growing up. Val always had a fascination and appreciation for her grandmother's penchant for fabulous accessories, unlike the other women in her family who, Val admits, may have been more on the practical side. As a child, Val spent hours lost in her imagination. Draped in all of Glamma's (as in *Glamorous Grandma's*—don't you love it?!) fabulousness, she wasn't a kid in grade school; she was royalty. And Glamma was delighted to confirm it. There were sunglasses, silk slips, scarves, brooches, and especially Glamma's colorful and soft-as-butter leather driving gloves in every color. When Glamma passed away, all of the things she had given Val over the years became that much more precious. When my team and I helped Val organize her home, we knew the gorgeous gloves, especially, needed the perfect spot in her closet. While she doesn't wear them these days, the acrylic box that is so appropriately *showing off* Glamma's gloves is her very favorite thing about the space. She still tears up when we talk about it. All those warm memories and feelings about her grandmother ignite in Val's heart when her eye catches those colorful pairs. In an instant, she's back in time with Glamma, giggling and twirling. When what we keep (and keep *out* on display) has great meaning to us, even the closet can be a little portal for magic.

AN ORGANIZED BEDROOM

The primary bedroom's ultimate purpose—more than any other room in the home—is for rest and restoration. Ideally, this is a spot where we can sleep deeply, a place where it's paramount to be able to truly relax and let your guard down. Walking into your bedroom should feel like an involuntary sigh of relief—this is your sacred space to be rejuvenated from the inside out. Yet collections of clutter—that can so simply be addressed and maintained—tend to steal the sense of calm a bedroom should offer. By adopting a few of my rules of thumb, however, you can reclaim this room as the most restful space in your home.

CLEAR THE TOP OF THE NIGHTSTAND

It can be tempting to abuse this handy piece of furniture, making it the depository for whatever you were too tired to take back out of the bedroom, from midnight-snack plates to hair clips. Resist the temptation! Think about it this way: the furniture closest to your bed, your prime spot for restorative rest or intimacy, should be as uncluttered as you want your mind to be before sleep. The only items I like to keep on the top of a bedside table are a reading lamp (if no wall light exists within arm's reach of the bed), an alarm clock, and a glass of water. Items to store inside a nightstand can include hand lotion, lip balm, an eye mask, vitamins, headphones, tissues, a notebook or journal, a pen, your current book, a charging cord, a small flashlight, and possibly a small jewelry dish if you take off your rings right before sleep. Whatever your inventory here, maintain organization by avoiding duplicates and storing only what you actually need or use right before sleep or upon waking.

STAGE YOUR GET-READY RITUAL ALL IN ONE PLACE

One of the key ways you can save time for the bigger moments in your life is by streamlining daily routines wherever possible. This includes saving steps by getting ready in the same place every day—I'm talking from underwear all the way to jacket and shoes and those finishing pieces of jewelry and accessories—and doing the reverse at the end of the day. If your closet is on the smaller side and your dresser is in the bedroom, the chest of drawers could be the anchor point for your get-ready ritual. Remember, the same tips for organizing any drawers in the closets apply to the dresser as well: utilize expanding drawer dividers and file-fold like crazy. Stackable accessory trays or a jewelry box on top of the dresser can serve as a safe place to deposit any jewelry you wear daily. Ideally the place you get ready for the day is also the same area you change into clothes for lounging or bed at the end of the day. Keep your laundry basket as close as you can to where you change. That way it's an easy (and immediate) dunk for the clothes you're shedding, and there's no temptation to "temporarily" drop them on the floor or bed.

WATCH OUT FOR DRAPING AND DROPPING

Maybe it's because entering the bedroom signals physical relief, and a place of to relax and unwind, but it can be especially tempting to drop and drape things as you come in or leave, rather than taking the three extra steps to put them away in their proper places. But as I mentioned earlier, this slippery habit is the fastest and easiest way to begin unraveling the hard work you put into creating systems or organization in your home. Items that you love, use, and need deserve a proper home, not to be tossed on the floor. If something's serving you, it deserves your respect and your care. That bedroom chair is meant to add coziness, provide a place to sit down and put on your shoes, or curl up with book for few moments. It serves none of these purposes when draped with the week's clothing or piled with bags and purses.

BE INTENTIONAL IF UTILIZING UNDER-THE-BED STORAGE

I like to encourage my clients that the space underneath the bed be kept empty under the same principle as to keeping a clear nightstand—facilitating an uncluttered mind for rest. But I also know that if your home lacks storage capacity, thoughtfully stowing items beneath the bed can be a practical solution. If you do need to utilize under-the-bed storage, treat it like you would any other storage space we've discussed: create zones and categories and contain items accordingly. There is a whole market for under-the-bed storage, and this is one place I recommend investing in products made specifically for storing, protecting, and accessing items under the bed, rather than repurposing boxes or bins of various sizes. While some of my studio apartment–dwelling friends with squeaky-tight square footage have successfully used under-the-bed storage for clothing and shoes, this space is typically best for storing items that you don't need access to on a daily basis, such as seasonal clothing, blankets, or extra linens.

CONSIDER WHAT YOU'RE KEEPING (AND KEEPING OUT) IN THE BEDROOM

Depending on the layout of and the space in your home, it's understandable that the bedroom may need to serve multiple roles in your life. If that's the case for you, do whatever you can to organize your space in a way that the most visible items support rest, relaxation, and intimacy. If you need to have a desk in your bedroom, be sure to have a drawer or other concealed spot to put away anything that could subconsciously kick your brain into work mode at the end of the day, such as your planner, laptop, or other electronics. You don't want the last thing you see before closing your eyes at night to be paperwork and bills. If your bedroom doubles as an exercise space, more power to you! Just be sure to have a designated spot (large decorative basket?) to stow workout equipment such as hand weights or a mat. Creating beauty around function is an important part of ensuring that your bedroom maintains the soothing vibe you need and deserve in your place of rest.

kitchen

CREATE SPACE TO SAVOR IN
THE HEART OF THE HOME.

I get so excited about all the possibilities that thoroughly organizing a kitchen opens up for individuals and families. And not just about how much more smoothly meal preparation and home operations will run when the space is streamlined, but about how much more connective the heart of the home will be because of it. So many layers of real *living* happen here. And as you bring new order and vision to this number-one spot to gather, make food, share stories, and nourish yourself and others, my hope is that you'll be able to savor it all more than ever.

COMMON PROBLEMS

With all the gathering, cooking, snacking, and living happening in this hub of the home, the kitchen is a natural magnet for an excess of clutter.

Not only does a lot of pass-through traffic in this space add to the chaos of misplaced objects and cluttered surface area, but I almost always find an overabundance of supplies and equipment that aren't in the right place to be useful or are simply taking up space and collecting dust. This excess in the kitchen is often a key sign that a "might need it someday" mindset is in play. And the question to ask yourself here is: Have you created a kitchen for your fantasy cooking or entertaining life, rather than one that serves you and your household in real time? Do you have a rice cooker but rarely make rice? Have you still never used that NutriBullet? Do you have an overabundance of Tupperware but no matching lids?

Add the daily bustle to the sheer amount of inventory accumulated in this space and you'll cue a second common emotional barrier: not even knowing where to begin. Between morning meal prep and hustling the kids into bath after dinner it can feel impossible to think about creating any order in this space beyond emptying the dishwasher and maybe throwing out the too-old leftovers. It's easy to say that you'll go back later to thoroughly clean out the fridge or organize the pantry, but that "later" often doesn't happen. And the more you have those moments over time, the more daunting the task eventually is, and the less prepared you feel to get started.

Don't get discouraged if you find that more than one emotional barrier is uncovered when it comes to organizing your kitchen. Most people have a clutter issue in this space (even if it's hidden behind cabinet doors). Start with one cabinet and keep moving. Some of the most common things I see that contribute to an overwhelming and underutilized kitchen space are:

- chaotic catch-all drawers
- dishes and glasses stacked precariously high
- overflowing utensil drawers
- Tupperware with no lids
- items shoved in cupboards
- tumbling pot-and-pan storage
- categories of items mixed together
- item placement that disrupts the kitchen layout and flow
- "dead space" in deep cabinets and corner cabinets
- seldom-used bulky appliances gathering dust

IDENTIFYING YOUR KITCHEN ZONES

Too often I find that kitchen items feel randomly placed, without rhyme or reason, much less a sense of flow or space efficiency. Identifying zones will help you make sense of your kitchen layout and get strategic with how you store and stock your kitchen inventory.

1. THE CONSUMABLES ZONE: This zone may actually be split into two areas: your refrigerator (for fresh food) and your pantry and food cabinets (for dry goods, oils, etc.).

2. THE NONCONSUMABLES ZONE: This zone contains storage for everyday dishes, including plates, bowls, glasses, and silverware.

3. THE CLEANING ZONE: This is the area that contains the sink and dishwasher (if you have one).

4. THE PREPARATION ZONE: This is where most of your food prep happens. This may be a stretch of countertop or a kitchen island (if you have one).

5. THE COOKING ZONE: This area contains the stovetop, oven, and microwave.

DISCARD VS. DONATE

After you've pulled everything out and categorized like items together for your new kitchen zones, don't skim over the process of deciding what to keep, discard, or donate. Perhaps you've never before made a conscious decision about what you want and need from this key space in your home—this is your time! Get honest.

The power of suggestion plays a huge (and often unfortunate) role in what we bring into our kitchens, especially when it comes to the latest and greatest appliances or nutritional fads. It's okay to let go of that bag of lentils that sounded really healthy but somehow you never reached for. Maybe you don't really care to make your own yogurt in that still-boxed yogurt maker after all. Maybe you don't enjoy cooking in general and would be happy with a smoothie for lunch and grazing deli-style for dinner most days. Great! Whatever your jam (I couldn't help it) is in the kitchen, own it. And *then* choose what stays and what goes accordingly. You'll enjoy the space—and *whatever* style of food preparation fits your lifestyle—so much more when you do.

If you're not sure whether something should be donated or just tossed, here are some suggestions to consider when working through your kitchen and pantry items:

Discard

- expired food, canned goods, or spices
- any food or kitchen item that no longer fits with your lifestyle or diet
- melted spatulas or cooking utensils
- scratched nonstick pots and skillets
- cracked or chipped mugs and dishes
- sugar that has clumped and hardened
- pasta that is more than a year old
- flour that is more than a year old
- baking soda that has been open for over a year
- canned vegetables that are more than two years old

Donate or Recycle

- unnecessary kitchen tools and gadgets (excessive amount of cookie-cutter shapes, apple and avocado peelers, etc.)
- unused or seldom-used appliances
- overabundance of dishes or Tupperware
- plastic storage bins and containers, if moving toward more sustainable products in your kitchen
- duplicate pots and pans, or appliances that serve the same purpose as ones you already have (i.e., let go of the rice cooker if you also have an Instant Pot)

Sometimes it helps us to let go of things when we know someone else would use or enjoy them more. Cooking schools, women's shelters, and organizations like the Boys and Girls Club can put kitchen items and appliances that are no longer serving you to good use. If you're getting rid of cookie cutters, for example, you might also want to see if your neighbor with the young children needs them. Thoughtful donations can be a great way to foster community and build relationships with the people around you.

jeneral guidelines
FOR PLACEMENT IN THE KITCHEN

THE CONSUMABLES ZONE

This is the area where your food is stored (i.e., your refrigerator and freezer area and cabinets containing food). All food should live in or near this zone along with the following food storage–related items:

- Tupperware
- storage containers
- plastic wrap
- parchment paper
- tin foil
- plastic bags

THE NONCONSUMABLES ZONE

Everyday dishes and/or nonconsumable items should be kept in easy-to-reach areas surrounding your sink, dishwasher or refrigerator:

Upper Cabinets

- plates
- bowls
- glasses and mugs

LIJ TIP: For small spaces or cabinet shelves that are too high, utilize risers to separate your dishes.

Upper Drawers

- silverware
- serving utensils
- cloths and hand towels
- small kitchen gadgets

decant & label

THE CLEANING ZONE

This is the space near your dishwasher (if you have one) and sink, where you clean up your mess after a meal. We typically keep these items under the sink:

- cleaning supplies
- sponges
- dish towels
- dishwasher detergent or pods
- trash bags
- gloves

LIJ TIP: A lazy Susan is ideal for keeping under-the-kitchen-sink items organized and accessible. This means no more layering of cleaning supplies; every bottle or container can have a "front-row" spot and be easily located.

THE PREPARATION ZONE

This area is the space on your counter or island where you do most of your cooking preparation. This could be chopping, baking, mixing, etc. These common items should be kept close by:

- cutting boards
- mixing bowls
- serving bowls
- graters, zesters, and peelers
- colanders and strainers
- measuring cups
- rolling pins
- cookie cutters
- whisks
- sharp knives
- mixing spoons
- mixing gadgets

THE COOKING ZONE

This area is where your oven, stovetop, and microwave are commonly found. Here, you want to utilize your lower cabinets and drawers to store all essential cookware and bakeware.

Different items belong in cabinets and drawers. Here's a quick breakdown below:

Lower Cabinets

- baking sheets
- pots and pans
- casserole dishes

Upper Drawers

- spices (if space allows)
- cooking thermometers
- spatulas and cooking tools

APPLIANCE HUB

This area will vary by a household's makeup and needs, but could include small appliances that are less frequently used or child-specific products, etc. Appliances often get shoved into the higher and hard-to-reach cabinets, making them a pain to retrieve and less likely to be used. Small appliances should be placed on shelves in a tall, pantry-like cabinet or in your lower cabinets. Whether these items make more sense in your preparation or cooking zones, the important note is to keep them together as your space allows.

- blenders
- waffle makers
- electric skillets
- electric mixers
- slow cookers
- toasters
- food processors

LIJ TIP: Utilize bins to keep all tools, cords, and attachments together with their respective appliances.

MISCELLANEOUS ZONES

With the space freed from purging all of your damaged, unused, and unwanted kitchen items, you likely have a little extra storage space at your disposal. That extra space can be used to find the best place for the miscellaneous items that might not fall into one of our kitchen zones. The main thing to remember is to keep all like items together and create a designated area for each category.

ON-THE-GO BOTTLES AND THERMOS STORAGE

Over the years, you've likely accumulated various water bottles and to-go coffee mugs from company events, restaurants, etc. A good rule of thumb is to keep only one to two water bottles and one thermos per person in a household.

THE KIDS' ZONE

If there are children in your home, you likely have a solid collection of bottles, sippy cups, bibs, and more. Keep these items separate from your main dishes, as your family will grow out of this stage before you know it, and then the space will be available for something else. A drawer in your island or an empty cabinet would work well for this zone, and in the case of a spill, you always want to know where the extra cloths and bibs are, for a quick grab.

space-saving tips
MORE THAN A DRAWER

With the right approach and products, one big drawer can serve as many storage compartments with definitive spaces for individual items.

USE EXPANDABLE DRAWER DIVIDERS

Adding expandable drawer dividers to any drawer that stores large utensils or multiple types of cookware is essential to maintaining an organized space. You can keep all your baking or cooking supplies in one drawer with dividers so that you can locate individual items easily and avoid jumbles and tangles.

USE MODULAR COMPARTMENTS

Your silverware is likely already stored in some type of compartmentalized drawer insert. When selecting your insert, make sure you pick something that best utilizes the entire drawer space and is suitable for the amount of silverware you have. I personally like the Bamboo Drawer Organizer Starter Kit from The Container Store—it comes with modular compartments, leaving room for your collection to grow or change. This is another great option for baking or cooking utensils in addition to the expandable drawer dividers.

USE DEEP DRAWER ORGANIZERS

Deep drawers are one area where our team typically finds people have not really implemented drawer compartments. What many don't realize is that you can save a ton of space by stacking things vertically rather than side by side. Deep, expandable drawer dividers are a great way to create smaller zones within the existing zones inside of your drawers. For instance, you could have all bakeware in one deep drawer, and separate the items into mixing bowls, strainers, and measuring supplies using dividers.

THE COFFEE STATION

The fact that this section of the book is dedicated solely to creating a mini coffee zone in your kitchen might say something about my (and many of my clients') collective love for a good cup of joe. Coffee equipment and grounds or pods can take up a good little chunk of kitchen space. But, if organized thoughtfully, creating a coffee station can simplify and add more ease to a comforting morning routine.

THE COFFEE DRAWER

Coffee-making supplies can take up a lot of space, especially if you use Keurig or Nespresso pods and have a variety of flavor options. A coffee drawer is an easy way to maintain organization of these items, making it easy for you to make a quick selection in the morning.

THE COFFEE CABINET

If you've put all your kitchen dishes and gadgets back into drawers and cabinets and still find that you have empty cabinet space, consider using an upper cabinet (preferably as close as possible to the counter area where your coffee maker sits) for coffee storage. Use the shelves to compartmentalize mugs, filters, pods, etc.

THE ULTIMATE COFFEE BAR

If your kitchen includes a built-in coffee machine or a separate built-in bar area, or if you have an unused section of your kitchen, don't be afraid to go all-out with fun canisters or glass jars for coffee beans and sugar, etc. Have fun creating a fully stocked coffee station that you and your guests can enjoy. Make it your own in-home version of that corner café you love.

BACKSTOCK AND ENTERTAINMENT

Do you love to entertain? Then you probably have lots of extra dishes and party and outdoor-barbecue supplies. If you have an overflow of party dishes, paper goods, and extra dinnerware for large gatherings, here are a few tips on where and how to store them:

- Store like items together. For example, if you have themed party supplies, you'll want to keep all of them together in the same location.
- Create bins for each theme: birthday parties, paper cups, plates, party napkins, and so on.
- Don't keep these items with everyday essentials. Find them a separate home.

SPECIAL-OCCASION AND CHINA DISHES

From wedding dishes to china inherited from family members, many of our clients have more formal dinnerware and serving dishes than they know how to store. If you don't use these items daily, find a home for them that is not in the kitchen. A dining-room cupboard, a sideboard, high shelves in your pantry, the hall closet, or even the garage—with proper protective dish-storage containers—could be an option. If you have empty cabinets in the kitchen after purging and reorganizing everything and choose to store your special-occasion dishes there, just make sure they're not taking up prime cabinet real estate or interfering with your cook zone.

OUTDOOR KITCHEN SUPPLIES

If you have an outdoor barbecue area or enjoy cooking outdoors, create a zone in your kitchen for outdoor dinner plates, napkins, and cooking tools separate from the rest of your kitchen utensils. Of course, this zone makes the most sense if the location is convenient to your outdoor cooking or dining area.

PARTY SUPPLIES

Party supplies are one of those categories that is really easy to lose track of over time. You may be surprised how much you've accumulated through

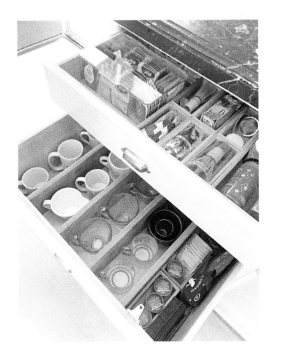

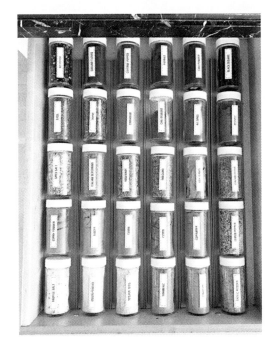

specialty drawers

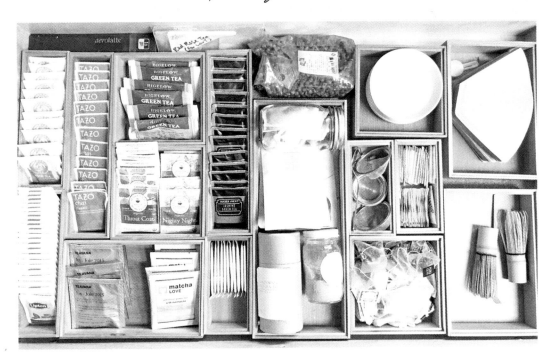

the years when you get it all together. While you're organizing your kitchen, this is the perfect time to gather all your disposable silverware, plates, bowls, and party napkins and create a designated space for them. A great solution, space permitting, is to create labeled bins in your pantry or a spare cabinet for these goods.

STORING SPICES

Spices often take up a lot of room in the kitchen. In many cases, you may have to create an additional space for them as your collection evolves. Here are a few different ways to store your spices—depending on your kitchen size and layout, you can decide which is best for you.

THE SPICE DRAWER

If you have an empty drawer near your cooking zone, this can be perfect for storing spices. Spice-drawer liner rolls are great here because they prevent the spices from sliding around in the drawer. The beauty of the roll is that you can tailor and trim each line to fit your drawer perfectly.

THE SPICE SHELF

If you have adjustable shelves within your cabinets or prefer to display your spices, risers are the way to go, allowing for easy visibility of each container. Add risers as your spice collection grows.

LIJ TIP: Check the expiration date on your spices and discard any that are out of date. Spices do lose potency over time. And what is the point of a flavor enhancer that has, well, lost its flavor? If you decant all your spices into matching bottles, label the bottom of the jar with the expiration date listed on the original packaging.

SPECIALTY DRAWERS

THE TEA DRAWER

If you have a generous amount of tea bags and an empty narrow drawer, bamboo drawer organizers will be your new best friend. The defined spaces they create will keep your tea-making supplies properly (and prettily) organized so you can always see exactly what you have and when it's time to restock. An acrylic tea box with compartments is a great option for this drawer as well.

THE SNACK DRAWER

Have limited pantry space? Designate an area for kids' snacks in a deep drawer and leave the pantry for adults! Compartmentalizing kids' snacks is a great way to offer your kids more autonomy during snack time at home and can save you a trip or two to the pantry when making your kids' lunches for school. Baskets are my favorite source of containment for this drawer.

BOWLS AND GLASSES

If your kitchen doesn't have upper cabinets or you have an excess of nicer dishes for parties and events, try stacking your bowls and glasses vertically in drawers. Again, bamboo drawer dividers create the perfect compartments for your dishes.

styling your kitchen
FUNCTIONAL BEAUTY

One key way to enhance your kitchen space without adding new clutter is to turn an item you already have on hand into an artful display. Try one or two of these ideas (but not all of them at once) to keep a clean aesthetic.

- If you have a large kitchen island, a pretty bowl or decorative tray can make a stunning centerpiece. And there's not much that beats the natural beauty of a vase of fresh flowers.
- Lean antique or decorative cutting boards against the countertop wall to add warmth and a personal touch without taking up space.
- Let fruit add color to your space. A ceramic bowl offering fruit never goes out of style. Just be sure to place it in an area that won't disrupt the cooking zone.
- If you have open wall space, try arranging your favorite cookbooks on floating acrylic shelves that leave the full covers in view. Beautifully designed cookbooks are perfect for adding a playful pop of color.

CENTRAL COMMAND

We've talked a lot about nourishment and feeding yourselves and others here. But the truth is, the kitchen is one of the most truly multipurpose rooms in the home. In addition to being the food hub, it often serves as the "ground control" of the home. Lots of daily transitions, comings, and goings happen in this space. Creating a kitchen command center (see pages 210–11) can help you or your family keep a visual of deadlines and responsibilities and stay in sync with the family calendar and activities. With an entryway/exit typically near the kitchen of a home, the kitchen is also often the last stop, and the last chance to grab small items, on the way out the door. A thoughtfully curated joy (not junk!) drawer (see page 229) can help with those last-minute needs.

THE PANTRY

While the kitchen is known as the heart of the home, I say the pantry is the heartbeat of the kitchen. And for a kitchen to flow and function successfully, it takes a well-organized and simplified pantry. From snacks to more hearty sustenance, everybody in the household is counting on and pulling from this spot.

CREATE ZONES FOR YOUR PANTRY

Zoning your pantry allows you to clearly see what food you have and what needs restocking. It also provides a better, more efficient method for putting groceries away, no matter who did the shopping. Everything has a home and it's clearly marked! Here are the steps to zoning your pantry.

1. In order to create the proper zones for your pantry, you need to determine the food and ingredient groupings that suit your lifestyle and diet. Take all items out of the pantry and group them together (on the counter, not in the pantry yet!). Use sticky notes or painter's tape to plan out your zones before putting the items back in.

   Here are some of the most common zones I like to create in pantries to get you started:

   Zone One: breakfast items
   Zone Two: snacks

Zone Three: condiments

Zone Four: pastas and grains

Zone Five: baking items

Zone Six: canned goods

Zone Seven: sauces and soup

2. Designate the appropriate zone for each category based on how often you use those items. Place items you use every day in easy-to-reach areas. Remember to leave extra room for growth.

3. Decide what containers are best suited for each category and place them in their bins.

4. Label your bins and put them in place, and place your items back in the pantry by zone.

DECANTING 101

When I first arrive on the scene in a home, most pantries house a mismatched jumble of oddly shaped boxes, containers, and packaging that either don't fit well on the shelves, don't keep your food fresh, or both. Decanting dry goods into airtight containers solves both of these issues, not to mention that it protects food from pests. Plus it makes it easy to see when supplies are running low and, by keeping items in containers sized to fit your storage areas, you'll be able to make better use of your space.

What to Decant

- flours
- sugars
- pastas

- nuts
- grains
- rice
- beans

- spices
- snacks, crackers, and chips

Steps to Remember

- Choose the appropriate-size airtight jar for the items you're decanting.
- Label the front or top of the container. Use a label maker or chalk or paint pens, which work great for this purpose.
- Write the expiration date on a piece of tape or use a label maker and place the label on the bottom or back of the container.
- If the item you are decanting requires instructions to prepare, make sure to write them on the bottom or back of the container. You can also cut out the instructions and tape them to the back of the container. (For example, on the rice container, write the cook time and the water-to-rice ratio needed.)

organizing SMALL PANTRIES

Not everyone has the glamorous walk-in pantry of their dreams. That's why I'm here! Even if your "pantry" is really a cabinet or a couple of drawers, any space has the potential to be transformed, both functionally and aesthetically. You simply need to add the right products and systems to make it work for you.

RACK AND CART PANTRIES

Two great options for adding pantry storage space to small kitchens are over-the-door racks and utility carts. Racks are an easy addition to any door, providing storage for your items without taking up space in the room. Carts can have bins of multiple depths, which make it easy to store containers securely and keep your items within their designated categories. When organizing pantry racks or carts:

- Zone items by level to the best of your ability.
- Use tall, acrylic containers for your baking supplies so that you can easily identify contents at a glance.
- Add labels on the top and the side of the containers.
- Make sure you select containers that have secure lids if you'll be picking them up from the top.

CABINET PANTRIES

Standard Pantry Cabinet (without Mobile Shelves) Tips

Here are some tips for organizing your pantry cabinet!

- In this type of pantry, staggering items behind each other is not functional for day-to-day finding, pulling, and replacing items. Instead, items should be zoned and placed in deep bins that are easy to pull down and have plenty of room for storing your items. In this situation, the bins serve almost like drawers.
- Again, place the most-frequented items on the most accessible shelves; it just makes life easier.
- Utilize lazy Susans, if space permits, for sauces, condiments, or canned goods.
- Don't forget to label those bins! This step will be especially helpful in a tighter, less flexible pantry situation.

Pull-Out Pantry Cabinet (with Mobile Shelves) Tips

Pull-out pantry cabinets can utilize all of the same tools as the standard pantry cabinet, but they also allow for a few more tricks:

- Since you are able to pull the cabinets out, there is more accessibility, so you can easily place items in the front and back.
- You can place the most-frequented items closer to the front of the rolling shelf and less-used items or backstock toward the back.

THE FRIDGE AND FREEZER

The refrigerator and freezer may seem like easy areas to skip when organizing because all the goods are conveniently hidden behind closed doors. But trust me, once you have an organized fridge and freezer you'll wonder why you never did it before. With labeled zones in place, putting away groceries, cooking meals, or even grabbing a snack gets a lot easier, and more pleasant too.

DETERMINING YOUR FRIDGE ZONES

By categorizing your food items into zones, you'll be able to create more storage, find things faster, and easily maintain order in a space where new inventory rotates in and out on the daily. These are the four typical fridge zones:

1. The cool zone: The area where your beverages, juice, milk, creamers, and bread go. Typically on the top shelf of the fridge.
2. The colder zone: The area where general cold foods like yogurt, deli meat, dips, leftovers, etc., go. Typically the second shelf from the top.
3. The coldest zone: The area where you should store your meats, fish, eggs, and poultry. These are typically best stored on one of the middle shelves.
4. Bins and drawers: Designated zones that have already been created at the bottom of most fridges. Place your salads, cheeses, fruits, and vegetables in these bins and drawers.

Things to Remember

- You don't have to put everything in the fridge! If you have an excess amount of soft drinks or water bottles, store your backstock in the pantry and replenish when needed.
- Label! To help keep your space organized, it's important to label any bins or containers so you can easily locate them, and remember where to put that next round of groceries.
- Implement the use of bins where you can for easy containment.

CONTAIN SO YOU CAN MAINTAIN

If your fridge doesn't have built-in compartments for your various categories, that's okay! These are our favorite bins to create your zones with:

Linus Fridge Bins Wine Holders

These are great for:

- water bottles
- wine bottles

Linus Deep Fridge Bins

These are great for:

- juice boxes
- kids' snacks
- dressings

The Container Store Fridge Organization Bins Starter Kit

These are great for:

- individual dips
- grab-and-go snacks
- salad kits

LIJ TIP: The two crisper drawers in your fridge are meant to store foods that perish more quickly. This includes fruits, vegetables, and leafy greens like spinach and arugula.

FREEZER SPACE SAVERS

Because the freezer is typically a smaller space, it can be tempting to simply tuck or shove things away. But there are sustainable and easy ways to contain your frozen foods too:

- *Utilize bins:* The same way you do in the fridge, use bins to separate your freezer food into categories. Compartmentalize!
- *Label:* Often, frozen foods are wrapped or packaged in a way that makes it difficult to identify them quickly. Items in the freezer are also often stored for longer periods of time, so there's a good chance you'll forget everything you stored over time. To avoid confusion, label not only your leftover bags and containers but also the bin you place them in.
- *Lose the boxes:* Keeping your items in boxes creates more work when retrieving food from the freezer. Empty items like waffles, popsicles, frozen rice, etc., into a designated bin for more convenient storage and easier access. Label inner packaging with the date you opened it.
- *File freeze:* Flattening your soups and meats in zip-seal bags before they're frozen is a great way to save space in the freezer. If you have pull-out freezer drawers, take your flattened bags of food, lay them down in your freezer until solid, then file them upright in drawers with like categories together. This method will save space and allow you to quickly and easily see what you have on hand every time you look in the freezer.

LIJ TIP: Avoid putting ice cream in the door. The door shelf is the warmest part of the freezer. Store ice cream toward the back of the freezer on the lower shelf.

KEEP IT FRESH: CHECK THOSE EXPIRATION DATES!

The perfect time to check for foods that have expired or have become freezer burned is after sorting and categorizing all of your fridge and freezer items and before placing them in your freshly cleaned and zoned appliance. Who doesn't love a completely fresh start? Once your new system is in place, it will be much easier to keep track of what needs to be used or tossed as you go.

kids' spaces

ORGANIZE IN SUCH A WAY
THAT KIDS ARE INSPIRED TO PLAY AND EMPOWERED
TO PLAY THEIR PART IN CLEANING UP.

I've always believed that thoughtfully organizing kids' spaces isn't just about preserving the sanity of parents or caregivers (though that would be reason enough!). The benefits of organizing actually have a lot to do with kids' well-being too. But I don't think I'd fully realized just what clear systems and structure could mean for a child and their belongings until after I'd organized nine-year-old Timothy's home. Timothy, a bright, energetic boy on the autism spectrum, and his parents regularly saw a team of professionals for help in navigating his diagnosis and seeking to provide increasingly better structures of support. As his parents explained to me, they wanted Timothy to feel an ownership of his toys and his room, but the clutter and chaos of his space after play, or simply after his daily routine, was really disruptive for him on both a physical and emotional level.

A few weeks after my team and I had finished organizing their home, Timothy's mom called me after an appointment with his therapist. She was in tears, but they were happy tears. She had just listened to Timothy tell his therapist how much he loved his room now, especially his play area, "because everything has a place." He could get things out and put them back in the right spot by himself now. And because—with the clear labeling—others in the household could do the same, Timothy knew exactly what to expect in his space every day, and that made him feel calmer and more assured. His mom shared that it was the biggest breakthrough they'd had in a while.

The truth is, aside from using both picture and word labels so Timothy could clearly determine which of his toys went where, we simply implemented the Life in Jeneral organizing systems and method that we would do for any family. It was a rewarding reminder that while every child's needs are different, structure can only ever help.

I treasure that victory for Timothy, and I believe that all kids can be a part of managing and maintaining their own spaces when everything they own, as Timothy so aptly said, has a place.

ORGANIZING THE PLAY AREA

Whatever the kids' play area looks like in a home—whether separate from or incorporated into a child's bedroom—I encounter many of the same problems:

- toys all over the floor, in every room of the house
- items shoved into the same bin without rhyme or reason
- messy, unkempt shelves
- toys getting lost easily
- no real clean-up routine
- piles building up in random areas
- tripping over toys

CATEGORIZING PLAY ITEMS

It may be a little meticulous up front, but with so many small parts and pieces making up a toy-filled play area, taking the time to pull out, categorize, and sort everything in the space is especially important in order to understand the full breadth of stuff your kids really have, and to identify duplicates. Key categories to help make sense of the mess are:

- stuffed animals
- dolls
- figurines
- books
- puzzles and board games
- coloring and art supplies
- building blocks
- cars, trains, and planes
- dress-up items and costumes
- bulky toys and sets

PURGING WITH KIDS

LET THE KIDS HAVE A SAY

After everything is sorted into categories and it's time to decide what to keep, discard, or donate—let the kids have a say in what stays or goes. Does that sound laughable? Like a nightmare waiting to unfold? You might be surprised. I've found that when it comes to play items, parents can actually be more sentimental than the kids when it comes to letting things go. Kids age out of or lose interest in toys, while parents can't help but feel nostalgic about those precious early stages and the items associated with those sweet memories of babyhood and toddlerhood.

GIVING BACK, TOGETHER: LEARNING TO DONATE

Encouraging your kids to help make decisions when purging the play area also gives them the chance to learn about donating and giving in general. Talk about donating as a means of giving away things that no longer fully serve you to someone who needs them or would use them more. You can explain that as kids grow, they become interested in new things, and old items can be handed down and fully enjoyed by younger kids, just as they had enjoyed them at that same age. In my experience, kids really do understand the vision their parents show them. And it's amazing to watch them begin to respond with surprising generosity. You can even include your children in the donation process by bringing them with you to drop off the bags with local charities and other organizations.

Questions to Ask Your Kids

- Which toys do you no longer play with?
- What do you think about giving these to someone else?

- Since you have two of these toys, what do you think about giving one to someone who may not have as many toys as you?

A PERSPECTIVE TO SHARE: Giving these items away will give someone else joy and give you more room to play with all of your favorite toys.

jeneral guidelines
FOR PLACEMENT IN THE PLAY AREA

Here's what I recommend for placement of your newly categorized items:

On Shelves

- books
- board games
- puzzles
- dollhouses
- stuffed animals
- display dolls
- bulky toys

In Drawers
(Make sure any items that aren't age-appropriate for your children are up high/ out of reach.)

- markers
- crayons
- scissors
- colored pencils
- stickers
- glue
- paint supplies
- beads
- glitter

In Baskets and Bins

- building blocks
- Legos
- small dolls
- Play-Doh
- train tracks

In Tall Baskets

- stuffed animals
- larger toys
- balls

Storage Systems or Pieces of Furniture

- puzzle racks
- dress-up clothes
- craft carts

ENGAGING KIDS IN CLEANUP

When you're exhausted and caught up in an endless loop of disorganization, it can feel like your only choices in wrangling a chaotic kids' area are either to "just do it yourself" and blitz-tidy the space alone for the billionth time, or to throw your hands up and surrender to the idea that it'll "just be this way for the next eighteen years." Believe it or not, I have good news for you on this front: once you have worked through the Life in Jeneral organizing method in your kids' spaces, you will be much better able to engage your kids in tidying up because, when there's a home for every item, putting things back makes sense and actually feels pretty gratifying.

Including kids in the process of cleaning up and organizing their own spaces not only teaches them to take responsibility for the messes they make, but also empowers them with a true sense of ownership of their belongings. Cleanup time doesn't have to drag. In fact, I think it can and should be the opposite. Don't you like good music when you're cleaning? So do most kids! Channel your inner Mary Poppins and, with a little imagination, snap, the job's a game.

MAKE A GAME OUT OF IT

Play pretend! Imagine their toys are sinking into lava and the princesses and action figures need to be rescued off the floor and tucked away. Or you can make cleanup time a friendly competition to see who can clean up the fastest and put everything back in the right place.

CREATE A CELEBRATION CHART

Create a sticker chart for all the chores the kids complete, including organizing their toys. Put small incentives in place that fit your lifestyle (i.e., if they earn a sticker every day this week for putting toys away, they get an

playroom magic

extra thirty minutes of playtime before bed Friday night and you'll help them clean it up . . . and so on.)

AND REMEMBER . . .

Cleanup time doesn't have to be perfect (this is a fun zone after all!). The kids likely won't put things away exactly as you would prefer, but the practice is what's important, and you can always jump in and help them if they seem to be struggling with the systems. My favorite part of engaging kids in cleaning up is that by including them in maintaining the organization of their spaces you're giving them a lifelong tool.

ORGANIZING YOUR SHELVES

COLOR COORDINATE YOUR BOOKS

Color coordinating books on shelves not only adds style and cohesion to a bookcase but is another great way to keep kids engaged in helping to maintain their space. When books are organized by their color family, it's easier and more fun for kids to put books in their spot. And book cleanup can be a game in itself as kids learn the order of the colors of the rainbow while they organize. Not to mention that before kids know how to read, they'll identify their favorite books by sight—so seeing the colors on the spine is actually a super helpful way for them to figure out what they want to read.

USE—YEP!—BINS AGAIN

Clear bins with lids are my favorite storage method for collections of toys and craft supplies in the play area. If your child is too young to read, they'll be able to identify the box where the exact toys they want are—both during and after play.

- *Collections.* Any sort of set or toy that comes with a multitude of parts and pieces should be contained as much as possible to keep all the components together.
- *Small pieces.* There's a reason there are so many comedy sketches with the parent stepping on Legos in the middle of the night, right?! Small-piece toy sets both are choking hazards and are easy to lose due to their size, so it's best to contain these in bins with lids. Think items like Play-Doh accessories, building blocks, Legos, and so on.

STYLE WITH BASKETS

- *Somewhat larger toys:* (balls, stuffed animals, larger figurines, etc.) that may not fit in bins with lids are best stored in open baskets of various sizes and shapes.
- *One-off toys:* toys that you only have one or two of and therefore don't necessarily need their own bin, such as a model train.
- *Frequently used items:* items that your kids want access to all the time; favorite special toys like stuffed animals, dolls, cars, etc.
- *Larger toys that can be contained:* balls, bigger-than-Hot-Wheels cars and trucks, baby toys, etc.

PUT IT ON DISPLAY

Of course, not everything can fit into a bin. There are larger, bulkier items that can't be properly contained in play areas, and this is perfectly okay! Use these as styling elements, putting them on display on your shelves. Group all display items together on one shelf if space permits.

arts & crafts supplies

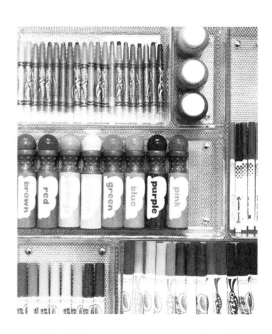

CRAFT-SUPPLY DRAWERS

Certain craft supplies are best stored in drawers, including markers, paper, and beads. While not everyone's arts-and-crafts area is in the same room as the play area, drawers in any space can be designated for kids' craft items.

SHALLOW-DRAWER COMPARTMENTS

Using modular compartments in shallow drawers to separate crafting supplies by type makes it easier for kids to put things back in their place after use. For school-aged kids, this is also a good place to store school supplies.

DEEP-DRAWER COMPARTMENTS

Maximize space and create structure in deep drawers with deep bins and cups to vertically store pens and pencils. Leave open space for larger crafting tools.

UNIQUE STORAGE SOLUTIONS

A CRAFT CART

If you don't have a designated play area, a craft cart is great for organizing all of your arts-and-crafts supplies in one mobile hub. Store the cart in a closet and wheel it to any room for easy access. Use the side bins for easy access to coloring books and paper.

PUZZLE RACKS

For kids who are crazy about puzzles, I love implementing puzzle racks. These vertical shelving units allow for stacking and storing a ton of puzzles and flat games in a configuration that takes up the least amount of space possible.

FLOATING BOOK DISPLAYS

Floating bookshelves that hang flat against the wall are a fantastic solution for making books accessible to kids without taking up space in the room. And they're great for keeping coloring books, workbooks, or early readers within reach as well.

CREATING KIDS' STORAGE THROUGHOUT THE HOME

STYLE BASKETS AND BINS IN THE LIVING ROOM
AND COMMON AREAS

Incorporating pretty baskets and bins that match your home's style into common areas makes it simple to tuck away toys after play and keeps those spaces comfortable and looking nice for adults too. And, more important, it brings your kids into family areas for play, creating opportunities for spontaneous fun with the family and making it a little easier to keep an eye on things while cooking dinner, etc.

CREATE A TOY CLOSET

Have any empty shelves in a common-area closet? Use them for bins or baskets of extra toys or kids' activities. It's a great way to make self-entertainment accessible to kids throughout the home without having to keep toys on display in your living spaces.

STORE TOYS IN THE GARAGE

If you have a garage, store toys that kids use outside (ride-on toys, sidewalk chalk, balls, larger cars and dump trucks, etc.) there. Garage shelves are also the best home for bulky toys that the kids are taking a break from.

ORGANIZING THE KIDS' CLOSET

We all know kids grow out of clothes and age out of toys so quickly! When you set up solid organizing systems within appropriate closet zones, they'll evolve right along with your kids over the years.

Common Problems in Kids' Bedrooms and Closets

- inventory that is constantly changing as kids grow
- inability to find things
- trying to force everything into a small closet
- inadequate storage for little accessories
- tangled hanging clothes
- piles building up on the floor
- messy shelves

CATEGORIZE AND SORT

Here's how I group items for a kids' closet:

- *Hanging clothes.* Categorize and sort into tank tops, short sleeves, long sleeves, dresses, pants, skirts, jeans, jackets, and sweaters.
- *Sweaters.* For sweaters you want to store on a shelf or in a drawer (as opposed to hanging), make sure you put them together and sort by color.
- *Folded and placed in drawers.* Categorize and sort undergarments, socks, tights, pajamas, swimsuits, etc.
- *Shoes.* Sort based on shoe type (e.g., athletic shoes, casual sneakers, sandals, dress shoes, school shoes, etc.).
- *Accessories.* This includes hats, sunglasses, purses, jewelry, hair accessories, etc. Categorize and sort into piles.

KEEP, DONATE, OR DISCARD

Here are some quick tips on knowing what to keep around—and what you should definitely be tossing.

Discard

- ripped or torn items
- discolored clothing
- stretched-out clothing
- stained clothing
- shoes with broken straps
- shoes with holes

Donate

- unnecessary duplicates
- old costumes
- free T-shirts that are not worn

DECIDE WHICH MEMORIES TO KEEP

It's been said that life with small children is made up of long days and nights but very short years. The tender ages pass by so rapidly, and perhaps that's why lots of parents can't help but feel sentimental about beloved childhood clothing items, stuff their kids especially loved or stuff they especially loved *for* their kids. If you can't bear to part with the onesie you brought your child home from the hospital in, or with that favorite teddy bear, by all means save them. But keep only the very favorite items and hold a high standard for what gets to go in the memory or keepsake box. Remember, the more you can hone in on the especially special stuff, the more prized and precious it becomes, and the more you'll remember it's there in the first place.

START A DONATION BIN

With how fast kids grow, something I've seen work well for managing the constant turnover of too-small clothing is keeping a donation bin in the kids' closet. Kids are so often outgrowing clothes and toys that a regular purge is encouraged to maintain organization.

jeneral guidelines FOR PLACEMENT IN A KIDS' CLOSET

ON RODS

Don't worry if your space doesn't allow for all items to be hung; they can live in other areas of the closet if space doesn't permit! Use rod dividers to make it easy to find items quickly. Typically, I hang:

- tops, blouses, and shirts
- dresses
- jackets
- jeans
- trousers and dress pants
- formal wear

IN BINS ON SHELVES

If the closet has a lot of open shelf space, consider storing these items folded on the shelves:

- sweaters
- jeans
- shoes
- hats
- accessories
- hand-me-downs for siblings

LIJ TIP: If you're planning on growing your family or have more than one child, add a designated bin to the closet for clothes your child has outgrown that you want to hold on to for the next child.

IN DRAWERS

Whether there's a dresser built into the closet space or one in the bedroom itself, these are the items that should be folded and placed in drawers:

- underwear
- socks
- tights
- pajamas
- swimsuits

space-saving tips
IN THE KIDS' CLOSET

Many of the methods to maximize space in an adult closet work magic in a kids' closet as well:

- *Switching to matching hangers.* And yes, space-saving slimline velvet hangers come specially sized for children's clothing too!
- *Categorizing and color coordinating hanging clothing.*
- *Creating compartmentalization.* Don't forget those expandable drawer dividers!
- *File-folding clothing.* Find tutorials at *www.lifeinjeneral.com*.
- *Using labeled bins and baskets* to store seasonal clothing, clothing to grow into, extra linens, memorabilia, and toys on shelves.
- *Utilizing an over-the-door rack* in small closets.

children's closets

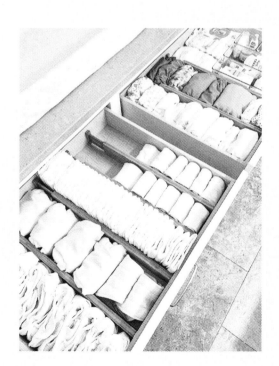

home office

EQUIP YOUR WORKSPACE, WHATEVER ITS FORM,
TO BETTER TAKE CARE OF BUSINESS.

You may not have a full room designated as a home office. Many don't. But whether you're working with a kitchen nook, a desk in a bedroom, or just a filing cabinet and a laptop, we're all taking care of the business of *home*—the bills, the finances, the communication—one way or another. More than ever, more people are taking care of the business of business at home too—working remotely, always adapting to our changing times.

Who would have thought we could spend this many hours a day on virtual video conference calls? Bless us.

Whatever your setup, simplifying and streamlining your home-office space will make a notable difference in how you feel about spending time in it, and, more important, how you feel about the tasks you're seeking to accomplish in it. When your office space boosts your confidence and inner calm, you won't dread the tasks at hand.

One of the big barriers when it comes to this particular space is the issue of time. And that makes sense—in today's shifting world, home is taking on a new meaning. For many people, that means trying to find a balance between work and home life. For others, who just need a quiet place to focus on bills and sorting out the family's schedule, the goal is still the same: a place you can focus on the task at hand. Only, the shifting environment can make it *feel* like you don't have enough time to do that, or that you should be prioritizing something else. You need to be able to create a space that clearly delineates the line between work and home.

Let's get everything *out* of the space that's distracting from your creativity and focus. And let's *add* anything you need to enter beast mode (is there a joyful beast mode?) when you hit this space. And, yep, I'm going to say it: Let's bravely face those piles of paper you've been avoiding for . . . awhile. You've got this.

CATEGORIZING YOUR OFFICE ITEMS

By now you know the drill. Pull everything out and group like items together. If you're having a hard time breaking down the categories in this space beyond the blanket "office supplies," here's a basic list of categories to help:

Clerical Items

- pencils
- pens
- markers
- Wite-Out
- highlighters
- Sharpies
- erasers
- glue
- paper clips
- binder clips
- calculators
- printer ink

Paper Products

- printer paper
- notepads
- Post-it notes
- postage stamps
- envelopes

Gadgets

- staplers
- tape dispensers
- hole punchers
- staple removers
- pencil sharpeners

Electronics

- desktop computers
- laptops
- monitors
- chargers
- cords
- printers
- scanners

ORGANIZING YOUR OFFICE DRAWERS

It's all too easy for office drawers to become junk drawers within which half the inventory is useless (or at least seldom used) and you constantly have to dig around to find what you're looking for. Remember my client with the ten thousand paper clips? Just because office supplies are useful doesn't mean you actually use them. Discard or donate the stuff you don't use, and

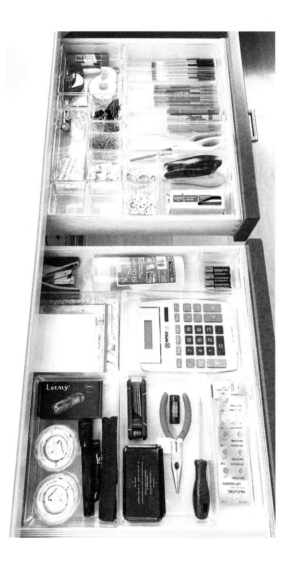

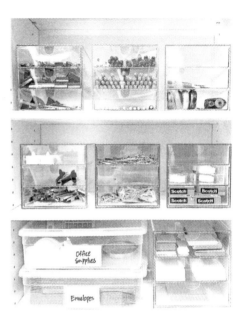

office supplies

then try these simple but smart containment tricks for what remains. There will be no more fruitless searching for your favorite fountain pens.

SHALLOW DRAWERS

Compartmentalization Is Key

Modular compartments are easily the best way to organize the clerical tools in your shallow office drawers. Depending on your style preference, I like using either Linus drawer organizers or wooden drawer organizers, because they come in various shapes and sizes, catering to your specific inventory and storage needs. Opt for individual compartment-organizers rather than a single unit with multiple compartments to truly customize your drawer to the exact supplies you want to store in it.

Ditch the Boxes

Keeping small items like paper clips and refill rolls of tape in their original packaging takes up extra space. Plus the thin packaging tends to fall apart over time, making a mess whenever you reach for the supplies within. Opt for smaller, uniform containers like the ones we mention above as a way to contain instead.

Coordinate Your Pens

Rather than putting all of your pens in one compartment, separate them into categories based on pen type, color, and usage.

DEEP DRAWERS ARE BEST FOR . . .

* bulky devices
* printer paper
* lined paper
* notebooks

ORGANIZING YOUR CABINETS AND SHELVES

Your home-office area may or may not have upper cabinets, and that's okay! These tips can serve as guidelines for any cabinet or shelf in your house that holds clerical supplies, paper storage, backstock office supplies, or photo albums.

CONTAIN, CONTAIN, CONTAIN

Determine the right types of containment for your office items based on the zones you created. Letter trays, document boxes, mail sorts, acrylic stacking drawers—anything that gives your inventory a permanent home and structure so you know exactly where to put it back.

LABEL

Label every drawer, every bin, every box, everything in that cabinet or on those shelves! (Remember, labeling not only helps you maintain your system for the long haul, it helps other members of your household return what they've used to the correct place, too.)

LEAVE ROOM TO GROW

If there's a particular category of office items that you know is guaranteed to expand, leave some space for growth. It's absolutely okay to (and even preferable) have empty space, as long as you have a system in place you can easily implement when new items are added in.

CREATING YOUR OWN WORKSPACE

If you don't have a home office space, but need one, a few steps and the right tools and systems can help you transform a small nook into a fully functioning and outfitted workspace:

1. Finding the spot. First things first: assess how much space you have for your makeshift or mini office, and where the best place to set up is.
2. Determining your purpose. What kind of work or projects will you be taking on here? Do you need to store clerical supplies and reference books or do you simply need a desk and a laptop?
3. Going vertical. My favorite hack! You honestly don't have to have a lot of room to create an office space in your home, especially when you utilize space vertically (build up instead of out). By adding shelving above (floating shelves can be inexpensive) a desk, a table, or counter space, you save a lot of surface area and square footage.
4. Investing in a cart. A rolling cart with drawer or bin storage is the ideal solution when you're creating a workspace out of a tight space or need your office setup to be mobile. When organizing supplies in a cart, apply the same containment guidelines we suggest for shallow and deep office drawers.

STOCKING YOUR SUPPLY CLOSET

If you have the storage, maintaining an office-supply closet (or set of shelves in a multipurpose closet) with backstock is recommended. You don't want to have to run to the store each time you need to create a new file or folder, you need an envelope to send a letter in the mail, or you run out of printer paper, especially when you're on a deadline! Additionally, many office items come in bulk (and can save you money when purchased that way), but it's likely not the most efficient use of space to keep it all in the desk area.

For containing items in an office-supply closet (a spot that's typically less visible in your home), I recommend using whatever you already have on hand rather than spending money on new products. When clearly labeled, empty plastic shoeboxes or old bins that you can empty out will work just fine for storing backstock:

The Best Office Items to Buy in Bulk

- printer paper
- file folders
- tape
- notepads
- pens
- envelopes
- staples
- printer ink
- label tape

ELECTRONICS STORAGE

For smaller electronics like cameras, hard drives, memory cards, and old tech, utilize bins and tuck them away in cabinets or a closet. Regardless of where you store your electronics, be sure to sort them by item and category so chargers and small attachments stay with their machines. After wiping the memory, consider donating outdated but functioning tech devices to charity. Nonfunctioning electronics can be recycled. Here are some of my favorite tricks to optimize your electronics storage.

CORD WRANGLING: TACKLING THE TANGLE

With all of the electronics and chargers that you need for a workspace to function, managing cords is a key part of the office-organizing process. Store cords in drawers with modular compartments to keep them separated and easier to access. For securing, put a tie or rubber band around the cord or wrap the end of the cord around itself and tuck it through to consolidate the length. Remember to label the compartments with the purpose of each cord.

GOING DIGITAL

Whenever my team and I begin tackling the office area of almost any home, one of the most common problems we encounter is that people have accumulated so much paperwork and photos over the years that they simply don't have the space to store it all. There is one resounding answer to this issue: it's time to go paperless and create digital storage files! If that sounds overwhelming and you're picturing yourself spending months hunched over a scanner, don't fret—there are lots of companies who specialize in converting physical files into whatever digital format you need. Here are a few of my favorites.

Digital Photo and Home-Video Storage

Legacy Box transfers physical photos, tapes, and VCR videos into digital files. See *www.legacybox.com.*

Online File Storage

Iron Mountain is a resource for people who want to transfer their paper file storage to digital. They provide a secure portal to scan, categorize, and centralize your filing system at *www.ironmountain.com.*

Kids' Art

Artkive (*www.artkiveapp.com) will* professionally photograph and digitize your child's loose pieces of artwork and then turn the images into a high-quality keepsake book. (See pages 231–32 for more on keeping or digitizing kids' artwork.)

Tips for Filing, Shredding, and Paperwork

- Physical documents that you may want to hang on to but won't need to reference more than once or twice a year (such as tax returns, deeds, leases, and signed contracts) should be filed in labeled folders.
- It can feel vulnerable to let go of physical copies of bank statements, medical records, and academic records, but rest assured that most organizations now have online portals where you can access your records digitally. After checking with your bank, doctor, or school to make sure that is the case, lighten the load in your file cabinet and shred the old documents.
- Shred any duplicates of paperwork and documents with personal identifying information, such as your social security number, bank account information, etc. If the initial purge of your home office includes ridding your home of lots of paperwork (first of all, YAY!), save yourself time and energy by hiring a mobile shredding service to pull up and take care of the "shred" pile.
- Recycle any papers that don't fall into any of the categories above and don't contain any personal information, such as junk mail, newspapers, magazines, and used envelopes.

CREATING A COMMAND CENTER

Whether you're a busy parent juggling school lunches, field trips, and managing the house and family schedules, or you work from home and need a place to organize your schedule, you may benefit from the use of a command center. Command centers are an LIJ essential when it comes to streamlining everyday routines.

- Having a visual of your daily responsibilities helps you to remember deadlines and activities.
- Seeing everything in one place helps your daily routine to run more smoothly so you can accomplish everything on your to-do list.
- Customization is key! Use certain colors or symbols to keep track of activities related to certain family members, helping compartmentalize everyone's schedules.

PLACEMENT

Hang your master schedule in your office space, inside your pantry door, or on the side of the island so it's at eye level for the kids—whatever location works best for your purposes!

CONTENT

You may not know exactly what information to include in your command center at first. That's okay! This tool, which is designed with a purposefully simple format, is meant to be tailored to your needs as they change and evolve. Use it to track work deadlines or strictly personal appointments, or to sync your entire family's activities. Add a checklist for the kids of what not to forget for soccer practice or dance lessons. You can even use it for weekly meal plans. Make it your own!

COLOR COORDINATION

If you have a hectic schedule and want to categorize based on event type or which child has an activity, create a system using colors. Use red for doctors' appointments, blue for afterschool activities, green for meal plans, and so on.

15

garage

TURN THAT BIG CATCH-ALL INTO SMART STORAGE
FOR WORK, PLAY, AND FAMILY FUN.

When I said earlier that I *always* save the garage for last and encourage every client I work with to do the same, I meant it. Why is this space such a beast? The garage tends to be a bit of a dump-all for (1) stuff that you don't have room to store in your home; (2) items you intended to discard, recycle, or donate, but never did; (3) objects you don't know what to do with and don't want to think about; and (4) bulky items from dozens of miscellaneous categories.

One of the big emotional blocks in this space is the issue of not knowing where to begin, which, yep, totally tracks. Garages tend to hold a *lot* of very different items, many of which you were probably hoping would secretly disappear if you stopped paying attention to them. (You wouldn't be the first person to hope for that.)

These issues exist in part because people see the garage as separate from their home instead of an extension of it. When you begin to view the garage as truly a part of your home, you'll treat it differently. And with the right systems in place, the garage not only has some serious storage chops but also the potential to serve your household in some really fun and rewarding ways. You just need to get intentional about the role you want it to play.

DETERMINING YOUR GARAGE GOALS

How your garage serves you and your family is limited only by your imagination. Whether you want to simply store your car, design a designated storage area, or create a workout space or workshop (or some combination of all of the above!) there are organizing systems to serve your purposes and make time spent here more enjoyable.

GENERAL STORAGE
This is an extension of home storage—not only a space to store your car, but also your tools, sports and recreational gear, outdoor equipment, holiday decor, kids' toys, and so on.

CAR STORAGE
This is straightforward car storage and storage of automotive accessories.

HOME GYM
This is a space where workout equipment is the priority, and vehicle storage less of one.

WORKSHOP

This is the craftsman's or handyman's paradise. It typically features a workbench of some kind and holds a variety of tools and equipment.

BACKSTOCK AND OVERFLOW STORAGE

This is storage for household-supply refills and extras from bulk purchasing.

LAUNDRY ROOM

This is a section of the garage that hosts the clothes washer and dryer along with detergents and other laundry-related products.

WHAT TO STORE IN YOUR GARAGE

Even once you've determined the main priorities for what your garage will store or what you'll use it for, it can still be tricky to wade through the amount of inventory you've collected in the space. After you pull everything out of the garage, make a list for yourself of what's most important for you to use in the space and then begin building your categories around that list. Once everything is sorted into categories you'll more easily be able to see what you have duplicates of and what can be discarded, donated, or consolidated for storage or use elsewhere:

Common Items Stored in the Garage

- vehicles
- bicycles
- scooters
- kids' cars
- wagons
- lawn chairs
- beach gear

- sports equipment
- cleaning supplies
- household backstock
- spare refrigerators
- tools
- electrical cords
- light bulbs

- ladders
- gardening tools
- lawn mowers
- seasonal decor
- memorabilia

Because most garages are not climate-controlled, the items stored within need to be able to tolerate humidity and sometimes extreme temperatures:

Items That Should Not Be Stored in the Garage

- clothing, bedding, linens, or plush toys (fabric items are susceptible to mold)
- flammable items (e.g., propane tanks, fuel cans, oil-soaked rags, etc.)
- food or beverage items that cannot withstand heat
- pet food (this is an invitation for pests)
- books or photos (these are susceptible to heat and humidity damage and mildew; see pages 230–31 for tips on how to store and organize photos)

PICKING A BIN

When deciding which containers to store items in, take into consideration which garage items are more vulnerable to the elements. Airtight bins and containers offer some protection from mildew- and rust-inducing moisture, while open crates are more convenient for keeping heartier outdoor toys easy to grab. Here are some guidelines for what to store in each kind of bin.

Airtight Containers

- tools that rust easily
- larger kitchen appliances that are used only periodically
- seasonal decor and lights

Clear Bins with Lids (Not Necessarily Airtight)

- workout ropes, bands, and weights
- household supplies
- cleaning supplies
- building supplies (extra tiles, etc.)
- memorabilia

garage storage

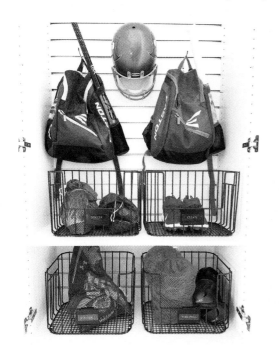

Open Crates

- sports equipment
- kids' toys
- beach toys
- household backstock items

general guidelines
FOR ZONING YOUR GARAGE

Zoning a garage can be daunting, but I promise that it's worth it! Here are some guidelines for making that space work for you.

HOUSEHOLD MAINTENANCE ITEMS

Store these items on higher shelves or stationary shelving units in an area you won't access often, saving prime real estate for more frequently used items:

- hardware
- light bulbs
- tools
- backstock supplies
- extra building materials

OUTDOOR GAMES AND BEACH GEAR

Keep these objects on the side walls of the garage so they can easily be transferred in and out of your car and back into place:

- sand toys
- beach chairs
- life vests
- ice chests
- umbrellas
- wagons
- ladder golf sets
- large Jenga blocks

GARDENING SUPPLIES

Store these closer to where you pull into the garage so they are easily accessible as you come and go:

- shovels
- rakes
- watering cans
- seeds
- gloves
- soil

BULKY OUTDOOR EQUIPMENT

Store large pieces of equipment like these near the garage door and as close to the garage wall as possible so that it's easy to take outdoors, but it doesn't get in the way of pulling your vehicle in and out of the garage:

- lawn mowers
- leaf blowers
- ladders
- motorbikes
- bicycles
- generators

SEASONAL DECOR AND MEMORABILIA

Since these items are used less frequently, place them on higher shelves or in overhead storage:

- holiday lights
- holiday ornaments
- yard decor
- tree stands
- flags
- wreaths
- birthday decor
- family memorabilia

SMALL SPORTING GOODS

Store these items against the walls (whether on a utility track or shelving unit) close to the car for easy retrieval and replacement:

- bats
- clubs
- rackets
- sports balls
- shoes
- mitts

FREE-STANDING STORAGE

Many garages are essentially boxlike structures with little to no built-in storage, which makes getting items off the floor a challenge. Free-standing units are game changers when it comes to adding storage capacity to a bare-bones garage.

OPEN SHELVING RACKS

One of my go-tos for outfitting an empty garage with storage capacity are metal free-standing racks with adjustable shelf heights. While the tall and wide shelves have room for bulkier bins and large storage boxes, the depth of the shelves means they take up little space in the garage when placed against the wall.

CONCEALED SHELVING

Don't have built-in cabinets? You can add them in yourself with free-standing tall storage closets. They're shallow enough that they don't take up too much space in your garage, but also have adjustable shelving inside that can be tailored to your needs.

ADDING WALL STORAGE

Garage wall space is prime real estate for storage. As an alternative to putting up shelving units that take up square footage, consider investing in a utility track to store your bulkier items and tools.

WALL HOOKS

Wall hooks make it easy to get a wide range of sporting goods and equipment off the garage floor. My favorite way to utilize hooks are the variously sized equipment hooks that attach to a utility track or a slat wall. Items to store on these hooks include:

- tennis rackets
- bats
- helmets
- beach umbrellas
- lawn and beach chairs
- golf clubs
- scooters
- strollers
- bicycles and tricycles

WALL SHELVING

If you don't have built-in shelving in your garage, a wall unit with floating shelves is ideal for storing boxes and bins of categorized items. Since each shelf's position on the wall and distance from each other is completely customizable, you can create a system that works specifically for your inventory.

CREATING CUSTOM SOLUTIONS

The beauty of an attached garage is really that, with a little customization, it can complement and fill in gaps for your home's setup. What kind of storage space does your home need and lack that you could create in the garage?

MAKE A MUDROOM

If your family is constantly on the go and your home lacks a good transition space, consider creating a mudroom in your garage. Add a combination of these elements and you'll have a new transition area to make coming and going with kids a lot easier:

- a bench or seating area
- extra storage space that's higher up
- bins and baskets for grab-and-go items
- cubbies or shelves
- hooks for hanging coats and backpacks

CREATE A WALL STORAGE UNIT

Have some free wall space in your garage? Maximize your storage capacity with custom wall shelving. You'll have the flexibility to change shelf heights, add drawers, and mix and match storage types to best fit your needs. Plus, the visibility of hanging items saves time digging through bins and boxes.

STORING BULKY ITEMS

Even those awkwardly sized items can be stored efficiently if you know a few tricks:

* nesting duffel bags inside suitcases so they don't take up extra space
* storing suitcases on their sides
* vertically stacking your larger seasonal storage boxes on top of each other
* placing less-used items on the highest shelves

LEAVE ROOM FOR LARGE TOYS

If you have children or grandchildren, you most likely have big, bulky toys around. Save garage shelf space for big toys to live on when rotating toys to hold kids' interest or while you're waiting for toys to become age-appropriate for younger siblings. Using customizable shelves allows you to change the shelf height and create room for larger items like baby activity centers.

WORK(SHOPPING) SMARTER

Perhaps no garage configuration has more small parts and pieces than the workshop, with all its tools. Keep the space organized with a few solutions for setup.

TOOL CARTS

Create a clear surface to work on by utilizing the space underneath it. Rolling carts are great for small tool storage, and they're compact enough to be tucked away underneath a workstation.

TOOL WALLS

Implementing a pegboard with hooks to hang your tools on the wall behind your work counter is a great way to save space and keep tools off the floor and out of reach for children.

TOOL DRAWERS

Maximize storage in workstation drawers by adding module compartments to shallow drawers for categorized tools, attachments, and the smallest of nuts and bolts. For deep bottom drawers, tall cups are essential for creating the most structure and function and capacity to keep like items together. No junk drawers here!

OVERHEAD STORAGE

If your garage is tight for space with little to no room for wall storage, don't forget to look up! Overhead storage is a great solution for seasonal items or things that won't need to be accessed more than once or twice a year. Make sure you measure the space so that it fits with the garage door lift components and the height of your car. Items that could be stored overhead include:

* bulky luggage
* holiday decor
* leftover building supplies
* larger beach equipment

PART 3

trouble spots
and how to
maintain

trouble spots
and solutions

SKIP THE CLUTTER SHUFFLE, DODGE THE DELAY
TACTICS, AND PART WITH THE PAPER PILES.

Some areas of the home seem to magnetize clutter more than others. I joke that a clutter magnet is any flat surface. And there are a *lot* of flat surfaces in a home. But joking aside, the fact that piles grow basically anywhere it's convenient to set something down tells us something. And *convenient* is the key word.

THE CLUTTER SHUFFLE

If you were to make a video of yourself moving through your home through-out a day, you'd see one long series of small decisions in which you had to choose (without really being conscious of it) whether you would take the extra steps to put something away in another area or whether you would set it down where you are, to "put it away later." It's such a simple concept, yet for a multitasking mind with competing priorities and limited time, setting each item down to deal with later feels like the easiest thing to do in the moment. Ironically, those "easy" choices compound to make our home lives so much harder. Instead of taking two steps to hang the jacket on the coat rack when we get home, we end up taking two hundred steps later just to gather and put away all the clothing items that have gradually accumulated on the backs of all the chairs and tops of furniture throughout the week.

If disorganization was a dance move, it would be called "the shuffle." Does this scenario feel familiar? You get home and, on your way through the kitchen, you set documents down on the kitchen counter because you just don't have time to deal with them at the moment. And then, a few days later, when you don't want to look at papers on the counter anymore, you move the stack to the dining-room table for a while. And then—when company's coming over for dinner—the pile finally finds a semipermanent spot on the home-office floor.

The problem with shuffling clutter is that with every transition you are losing time, energy, and space. I know that you can't always drop what you're doing to spend the thirty-plus minutes to read and file those documents, but what if you took them straight to the paper tray on your desk and put a little reminder in your calendar, blocking off thirty minutes to get the reading knocked out later this week? By taking the extra ten steps to the office, by being intentional with where we place our things the first time, we save ourselves the annoying limbo . . . and it just might be a little less stressful and more delightful to have friends over for dinner too. Here are other surfaces to watch out for clutter creep:

- entryway benches or mudroom counters
- the tops of front-load washers and dryers
- pantry floors
- bedroom floors and chairs
- nightstands and dresser tops
- closet floors

THE JOY DRAWER

While it's not a surface, there's one small space that is so adept at magnetizing clutter that it was named for it: the *junk drawer*, of course. To be honest, I would really like to ban that term from the family vernacular. While most of us do need a small space (preferably in a highly trafficked area) for miscellaneous but frequently used items to live, this little tool-box- or command-center-in-a-drawer should hold the opposite of junk. It should be the spot that has exactly what you need, when you need it quickly. That's a good feeling, and it's why I've renamed this spot in the home the *joy drawer*. It might seem silly, but I think what we call things carries intention whether we realize it or not. I want more joy in every home. And, obviously, less junk.

How can you take your drawer from junk to joy? Follow the Life in Jeneral method for sorting, purging, and containing, and then restock the drawer only with frequently used items you'd like to be available at a moment's notice, such as:

- utility scissors
- batteries
- a flashlight
- Scotch tape

- measuring tape
- rubber bands
- two to three pens
- small notepad

- Sharpie markers
- stamps
- checkbook

PAPER-TYPE PROBLEMS AND SOLUTIONS

It's always the paper-type piles that are stickier and trickier than other types of clutter. Paper holds things with meaning—ideas, messages, memories, and art—which can make it harder to know what to do with it. And while you're trying to decide, the piles only grow in quantity, and the task of organizing them becomes even more daunting, and so you postpone . . . and so on. But even for the most sentimental of paper categories, like these two below, the solutions might be more straightforward than you think.

ORGANIZING PHOTOGRAPHS

Photographs are the one thing I recommend that you save to go through *after* you're finished organizing the rest of your home, lest you be dragged down into a nostalgic or bewildering (whose photos are these again?) abyss that you can't pull out of. Put a large bin in a safe (climate-controlled) space and then, as you come across photo stashes while purging different rooms in your home, put all the photos in the bin (without stopping to look through them). Then, after the rest of your home is how you want it, you can dive in.

Not only do you most likely have troves of your own immediate family's photographs, but you might have boxes of images passed down from your parents that were passed down to them from family members you've never known. Whatever your collection, here's what to do:

Discard

- duplicates
- blurry images

- images of people you can't identify

- photos of travel locations with no people you know in them

Store

If you don't want to use photo albums but want to save the images, place them in acid-free archival storage boxes, labeled by year.

Digitize

To save space while preserving your memories, consider having your hard copies scanned into digital files. Before you send to a professional service (like Legacy Box), organize them chronologically, even if you have to guess at the years. That way there will be some sense to the order of the images when you receive the files.

As you're sorting through your photos, if there's one that makes your heart jump immediately upon seeing it, may I recommend that you go ahead frame it or put it somewhere on display? If the image brought you that much joy in an instant, don't leave it in a storage box. Let it serve its purpose.

DEALING WITH KIDS' ARTWORK

Kids create art constantly. It's spilling out of their school backpacks. It's taped to the wall in whatever area you deemed safe enough for fingerpainting in your home. It's covering the fridge. And there may even be boxes titled JOEY'S ART FROM—GRADE X stashed up in the attic for safekeeping. Even though the kids are mass-producing the stuff, it can still be hard for parents or caregivers to let it go. We worry:

- it will hurt their feelings if they find out you threw it away
- they put a part of themselves into their art
- they made it "just for you"

- they're growing up too fast and these pieces represent a precious stage
- they might want it someday (I have *not* found this to be true. Adult children rarely want their childhood artwork. But I have worked with parents who have told themselves this fib because *they* want a reason to keep it.)

I completely understand why parents want to remember the art their child made from scratch in those tender years. The problem lies in *how* it is saved and how much. A few tips on treasuring your child's art:

- Like with the childhood-memorabilia box concept, condense your collection to one bin of your *very* favorite pieces. You'll love them even more for it. (I had a client with ten large plastic bins of her children's artwork throughout their school years. It took up an entire closet—hard to really enjoy it that way.)
- Frame a few of the neatest pieces for wall decor in any kids' spaces in your home (or anywhere you want to add color or a playful vibe). The kids will be proud.
- And my favorite option: utilize a service like Artkive, which takes professional photographs of the artwork and creates an archival-quality keepsake book with the images. Besides the physical space this saves, what I love most about this solution is that the final product—a piece of art itself—encourages you to actually sit down and *look* at it with (or most likely without) your kids. This is so much better than the art sitting in storage and never being seen or enjoyed.

A single cluttered surface or trouble spot may not seem like a big deal on its own, but all the surfaces added together make for a cluttered life. By taking these extra steps in the present, you're choosing a joyful future over the convenience of the moment. And time after time in my work, I've seen that the biggest impact in achieving an organized life is made in the small, daily decisions.

solutions for trouble spots

how to maintain
for life

SHOW UP FOR YOURSELF
THROUGH LITTLE, LIFE-GIVING HABITS.

Once your home has been organized and systems are in place, the method for maintaining order is fairly straightforward: Put it back where you got it. Yep, it sounds simplistic. But, man! So much hinges on that commitment to simply returning things back to their correct homes after use. I always tell my clients: Invest in truly organizing your home once and you'll never have to do it again. And that's true. When you put good systems in place in every space, the foundation for keeping your home organized is set forever. But there's a significant caveat to this guarantee: your home will not stay that way if you don't commit to the work of maintaining, the small day-by-day actions that add up to big lifestyle change.

IT'S THE LITTLE (DAILY) THINGS

Developing small daily habits and routines like these can save you from spiraling, and maybe, over time, become joyful acts of disorganization defiance—your way of showing up for yourself:

- *Making the bed.* This simple act has a near-miraculous ripple effect when it comes to setting the stage for your day, and, apparently, your life. Do a quick internet search for "How making your bed can . . ." and you'll be inundated with stories and studies that show how bed-makers are happier, healthier, and more successful.
- *Hanging things back up upon arrival.* The coats, keys, backpacks, bags, market totes—resist the urge to set them down or drape them over furniture. The time spent on "hanging it up later" multiplies like bunnies.
- *Not setting the mail down after retrieving it.* Flip through it while you're walking into the house and stand over the recycling bin to purge. For mail that really does need to go in a respond-to- or pay-later slot, keep the receptacle small.
- *Committing to cleaning up the kitchen after dinner.* There's something about walking into a clean and clear kitchen in the morning that makes you feel like the new day is doable. I know the after-dinner hour can be a tricky time for parents of small kids. A friend of mine and her partner set up an evening system where one does kid bath and story time while the other runs kitchen cleanup. Then they switch roles the next night.

- *Keeping a fifteen-minute evening pick-up routine.* This is another reset hack for breathing more easily in the mornings. Keep this tidy time brief on purpose. It's not about making the house pristine, and you time, cuddle time, or downtime before sleep is part of what makes living sweet. Set a timer. Make it a little race with yourself or get the family involved, and then call it "good enough!"

The bedrock of maintaining an organized home is consistency, committing to regular (and I hope joyful) practices in our homes and in our minds. And it's about celebrating progress, not perfection!

WEEKLY RESET

One of my favorite parts of the week is Sunday afternoon at home. It's when I turn up the music, run a load of laundry, make sure my morning-coffee supply is stocked, and look at my calendar so I know what's coming in the week ahead. If the floor needs mopping or there's a chore that requires a little more time than I have to give during the workweek, this is when I do it. It may be simple, but this weekly reset makes all the difference in how I feel about . . . well, almost everything. Yes, I'm taking care of my home and responsibilities, but by safeguarding this time, I'm mostly taking care of me. Whatever form it takes, I hope you'll find your own version of a weekly reset. It's bound to become one of your favorite rituals too.

RETHINKING HOW YOU CONSUME

Having an unencumbered home doesn't just depend on managing and tidying what we own, it means rethinking how and what we bring into our homes, as well. Two life-changing philosophies:

- *Buying quality over quantity.* Buying fewer but higher-quality things usually isn't more expensive in the long run, and can help you be more thoughtful about what you select. You'll end up with items you can enjoy for a long time, which is both great for you and good for the planet too. When making purchases, think about what items you purged most in each room when organizing your home, and let that guide what you choose to buy in the future.

- *Giving experiences over stuff.* On birthdays, holidays, and special occasions, surprise family members with a trip to a traveling art exhibit, a concert featuring their favorite artist, or lessons for a new interest or hobby. I love this practice of gifting experiences not only because it brings less clutter to deal with into our homes but also because it fosters deeper connection with each other: something fun to do together, and even better, something fun to talk about together.

LISTENING TO YOUR GUT

So how do you catch yourself before sliding back into old habits of disorganization and old ways of thinking? Keeping an eye out for clutter creep in your typical trouble spots is certainly part of it. But, like with everything we've touched on, there's also an intangible element to it that may be an even better indicator that it's time to check back in on the organizational health of your home and lifestyle. Remember way back at the beginning of this book when we first talked about that deeply settled type of happiness? After you've worked through the process of thoroughly streamlining and organizing your home, you most certainly are going to experience that rich, one-of-a-kind, rest-in-your soul feeling of deep satisfaction. Pay attention if and when you begin to lose that feeling. If a sense of unease begins to creep back in, it's time to take another look inward—what old emotional barriers might be kicking in? It's never too late to flip the script on them again. And you are worth it every time.

MAKING ROOM TO GROW

Over time, the needs of our homes will change because we as people are constantly changing too. Not only do kids grow out of both clothing sizes and activities faster than we can blink but even as adults, our likes and hobbies keep evolving through the years. And thank goodness, as that's what keeps life fresh! But what does growth mean for the organizational systems you put in place throughout your home? The great news is that—while labels may change—the foundation you set through the Life in Jeneral method will last. As your kids' activities change from playing with baby dolls to jewelry-making in the playroom, or as they outgrow those yogurt and applesauce pouches in the fridge, you'll write new labels and perhaps switch around the size and type of containers you use to work for new items or new categories that are needed, but your systems can adapt right along with you and your family.

In the meantime, leave a little space for growth in the present too. That can look as simple as buying a full set of groceries before you organize your fridge or pantry and then still reserving a little shelf space for backstock or extra items. The bottom line is that you've done the hard work of laying a foundation, and now you get to enjoy the journey.

CONCLUSION

As we come to the end of your consultation on this organizer's couch, what you may not have known is that, this whole time, there were dried-up cake crumbs in between the cushions. I'm a work in progress too. I'm still learning to be present in this one precious life.

What I do know is that I love this work. I feel so lucky to get to witness the transformation that organizing a home can bring. It looks like freedom. It looks like empowered individuals and deeper relationships. It looks like people getting excited about their lives again.

Want to know what it doesn't look like? Perfection.

I'd like to go on record about something (which, it turns out, a book is really handy for): what matters most in this life is *not* pictured in all the perfect-looking, gorgeously curated, and brightened-up images on any organizer's social media account, including Life in Jeneral's. Yes, I adore getting to bring beauty and function together. I like that we can have fun with these platforms and give each other artful, aspirational boosts. But I never want to confuse a perfectly ordered and styled home with the key to happiness, success, or fulfillment.

Real life is gritty and disheveled: full of dirty dishes, sometimes-grumpy humans, dog tracks on the rug, and seasons of grief where you wish you could just put it all on hold for a while. Even the most beautiful, breathtaking parts of this life (of which there are so many) are imperfect. And maybe that's how they're meant to be.

What I hope you find through the soul work of organizing your home is that you're simply creating a more gracious space to hold it all, including yourself. This work is about building in the breathing room so that when it all *does* go sideways, you're more able to bounce back.

More than anything, what I want you to take away from this time together is hope. Hope that—no matter your story, upbringing, or circumstance—you can create a home and life where you feel freer to focus on whatever brings you the most joy.

Want to know something encouraging? You were made for this. Made for this life journey. Innately made for deeper connection and purposeful living. Even made for the soul work it requires to get there. You just have to choose to keep your heart open along the way.

Friend, you have the tools to do this work. You have everything you need to make space in your home and life for what matters most to you. And you can start today.

ACKNOWLEDGMENTS

To my collaborator Charis Dietz, for every call, text, voice memo, and every second spent on this book alongside me. For listening to every story and truly hearing my heart in it all. For creating magic within these pages and your incredible talent. For turning into my soul-sister. Without you, there would be no book.

To my editor, Anna Montague: thank you for reaching out, hearing my voice, and for understanding that this book needed to be made. Special thanks to the whole team at HarperOne, including Judith Curr, Gideon Weil, Adrian Morgan, Lisa Zuniga, and Lisa Sharkey.

To my agent, Whitney Gossett, for being the connector to everyone who made this book happen.

To my brand managers, Lewis Kay and Carly Morgan, for believing in me from day one and taking a chance on me. I am forever grateful to you both

To Mama Ro, Sally, and my nephew Declan. I love you more than you will ever know.

To my brother Dre, for loving me through all my crazy ideas and never complaining about the countless hours you have helped to get me to them. I love you and know Dad is so damn proud of us.

To the love of my life, Dan. For loving me through every late night and weekend spent writing. For telling me every day how proud you are of me, and for being my biggest supporter, especially during this past year. I can't wait to spend the rest of my days doing life alongside you.

To my Life in Jeneral team, for every day, every home, and every life we have changed. You've become family, and I am forever grateful.

Finally, to my clients. You have opened not only your homes to me, but also your hearts. Your trust inspires me daily. This book is for all of you..

RESOURCES

Keep making space for what matters most . . .

Whether your journey in organizing your home has just begun or you've been at it awhile, I want to continue to be a resource to you along the way. At *www.lifeinjeneral.com* you'll find a comprehensive hub of fresh and updated resources at your fingertips, including product recommendations, video tutorials, tips on organizing specialized spaces, and so much more. And follow *@lifeinjeneral* on Instagram for your daily dose of positive organizing energy and inspiration. I can't wait to keep growing with you!

ABOUT THE AUTHOR

JEN ROBIN is the founder and CEO of Life in Jeneral, a full-service organizational design company that believes transformation begins at home. Jen is also the founder of LIJ Spaces, a custom cabinetry line designed from the unique viewpoint of a professional home organizer.

Jen has always loved organizing and creating systems. She started out as a celebrity executive assistant, where she mastered the art of to-do lists, time management, and efficient systems. In the process, she realized that organizing truly was about helping people realize what they want—and what's holding them back from achieving their purpose.

Over the years, Jen has successfully evolved Life in Jeneral into a holistic home transformation company. With an eye for design and a knack for creating function in any space, Jen and her team are teaching people to marry organization, function, and aesthetics so they can live a more joyful life. Since Life in Jeneral's inception in 2014, Jen has applied her systematic and soulful approach to clearing the stress and clutter from thousands of people's lives.

She lives in Los Angeles, California.

HarperCollins books may be purchased for
educational, business, or sales promotional use.
For information, please email the Special Markets
Department at SPsales@harpercollins.com.

FIRST EDITION

Designed by Bonni Leon-Berman

Photographs © Jennifer Robin

Library of Congress Cataloging-in-Publication Data is
available upon request.

ISBN 978-0-06-308150-5

21 22 23 24 25   LSC   10 9 8 7 6 5 4 3 2 1